WHAT I SAW GOD DO

Reflections on a Lifetime in Missions

DAVID M. HOWARD

Foreword by Leighton Ford

Copyright © 2012 David M. Howard
All rights reserved.
ISBN: 1479180386
ISBN 13: 9781479180387

Dedication

TO THE MEMORY OF MY PARENTS

PHILIP E. HOWARD JR. and KATHARINE G. HOWARD
who prayed, influenced and encouraged me
to a lifetime in missions.

Acknowledgements

It is customary for an author to express special thanks to those who have contributed in getting his book written and published. I am in a dilemma because friends and family have been urging me for twenty five years to write this book. I cannot possibly acknowledge, or even remember, all who had a part in this.

Therefore I will limit this to acknowledge several who have been especially instrumental in bringing this effort to completion.

The late Virginia Muir, former Managing Editor of the Tyndale Publishing Company, was my first editor who encouraged and advised me for several years in the initial stages. I am deeply grateful for her expert help.

Roger Palms, former editor of *Decision* Magazine of the Billy Graham Evangelistic Association, has guided me in the final stages to bring this book to completion. It has been a joy to have his professional and friendly participation.

My wife, Janet, has followed through with continued stimulus and detailed copy editing of the manuscript. I am deeply thankful for her love and help.

Introduction

For many years people have urged me to write some of the stories they hear me tell. God has allowed me to see His hand at work in many parts of the world. They also feel that God has gifted me in storytelling. Therefore the time has come to share some of these stories more widely.

It is true that I have been involved in missions for more than half a century. I was part of the post World War II generation of missionaries, graduating from Wheaton College in 1949 and going to the mission field in 1953. Thus I have been privileged to see God's hand in missions since the mid-twentieth century.

Some friends, such as Dr. Lon Allison, director of the Billy Graham Center at Wheaton College, as well as others, have suggested that I write as an observer. Others have stressed that I was also a participant and have thus been both a participant plus an observer of mission movements for sixty years. This has given me a platform from which to write about the trends, events, and people I have experienced and known. This is my reason for writing.

Foreword

Many years ago I read Eugene Peterson's *A Long Obedience in the Same Direction,* a classic description of the journey of discipleship.

I thought of that title as I read my friend David Howard's reflection on his own life. It has been *long* – from his very young days to now. And *obedient* – as he has sought to follow the Lord. And *in the same direction* – always focused on the church's great task of making Christ known.

I met Dave my first year at Wheaton College, where he was a graduate student, and also recruiting students to have a passion for what was then called "foreign missions". As I recall Dave asked me to be involved in promoting the cause, and I agreed – but don't think I followed through very well!

Dave I think first knew me from a distance because I was part of a group of guys who met to pray every afternoon just before dinner over the Alumni Gym. He says he didn't know all of us but that our prayers were very loud!

Later our paths crossed many times, and more than once converged. We worked closely together when he directed a major consultation in Thailand sponsored by the

Lausanne Committee of World Evangelization of which I was chair. My admiration for him began early and has never waned.

In this collection of memories Dave has given us concrete examples of how our stories – the stories with a small "s" – connect with God's story – the story with a large "S" of what God is doing in the world.

Small slices of life – in a godly family, summers on a farm, study at college, in pioneer missionary treks, engaged with the global church – should encourage all of us to realize that the Lord uses what sometimes seem like very ordinary happenings to work out his purpose for our lives. As Dave looks back on his own life we can see how a "long obedience" counts more than we realize at the time.

David Howard's account is a living example of the apostolic calling God gives to each of us – *the work of faith* (and he learned to work hard on the farm and the mission field); *the labor of love* (and what else could keep him going through some very difficult times); and the *steadfastness of hope* (for he saw God work in what must have often seemed like impossible situations apart from God's amazing grace).

No doubt friends and family will read these stories. And I am sure others like myself who have known and worked with Dave will too. But I also hope many younger leaders will read this – they may not be familiar with the times in which he lived – but they will most surely be inspired by the life he has lived through these times by the energy with which Christ worked in him!

Leighton Ford
Charlotte, North Carolina

Table of Contents

Prologue 1

SECTION ONE: EARLY OBSERVATIONS

1. The Day I Met George 5
2. A Young Patriot 9
3. The Yum Yum Lady 15
4. My Father's Hands 19
5. Grandpa Howard and Me 23
6. A Tale of Two Spinsters 27
7. The Pleasure of Hard Work 31
8. The Place of Good Books 37
9. Toronto 1946 39
10. A Man and His Influence 41
11. The Discipline of Sports 43
12. He Never Raised His Voice 47
13. The German Submariner 49
14. "It's O.K., Sonny Boy" 53
15. The Love of My Life 57
16. That Special Time of Love 61
17. Phyllis: Her Ministry to Children 65

SECTION TWO: OBSERVATIONS OF A MISIONARY

18. The Lord Used You in My Life 71
19. All Your Needs 73
20. Eliphaz: A Confession to Make 77
21. What About Honoraria? 81
22. The Picture Bible 85
23. Our Lives in Santo Domingo de Heredia 89
24. Explosion of Short-Term Missions 93
25. Please Don't Rob Me of that Blessing 97
26. The Outreach of Agustin Ramos 101
27. Struggles of a Witch Doctor 105
28. Victor Landero: A Remarkable Man 107
29. My Hatred of David Howard 111

SECTION THREE: OBSERVATIONS OF A WORLD MISSIOLOGIST

30. The Many and the One 117
31. Urbana – Threats and Prayers 121
32. Sold Out to Satan 125
33. The Influence of a Faithful Man 129
34. Just Before I Jumped 133
35. Trends in Missions 135
36. Those Bible Notes 139
37. Arrested! 141
38. The Bombshell of Lausanne '74 145

39. The Elephant and the Crocodile 149

40. Another Man in His Cell.. 151

41. I Was Saved in a Bar.. 155

42. The Danger of Twisting Scripture... 157

43. A Timely Phone Call... 159

44. Mission Life Then and Now... 163

45. On Being a WASP... 167

46. We Are Who God Made Us to Be 171

47. The Place of Laughter 175

48. Asking and Answering Questions... 179

49. Oh, For a Tape Recorder 181

50. "In the Garden"... 185

51. Is There Room for Two? 187

52. God's Encouragement to Me.. 189

53. Changes in Missions.. 193

Index - Some of the Books That Have Especially Influenced Me 199

Epilogue 207

PROLOGUE
Then Came the Flames

Chaudhry was a fanatical Muslim, a freedom fighter of the Free Peshawar Army in Pakistan. He had been taught that he could honor Allah by killing non-Muslims, or those whom he called infidels. Consequently, as a captain in that army, he had opportunity to kill Christians when he found them. When I was visiting with him in Pakistan he told me the following story.

One time he took a contingent of soldiers with him to a small village where he went looking for Christians. They asked around in the central plaza of the village for any Christians who lived there. They were told that, yes, there was one family that lived up the road. They pointed out the house. Chaudhry took several heavily-armed soldiers with him and they went to the indicated home. When he knocked on the door a man and a woman came. Chaudhry asked them, "Are you Christians?" Their answer was affirmative. So he replied, "Then I have come to kill you." This, of course, was startling to them and they were shaken for a moment. But just then their ten-year-old daughter stepped around in front of them and stood between Chaudhry and her parents. She turned to him and said, "Captain, if you are going to kill us, please give us permission to do something first."

When he told me this story he said that he became irritated that this little girl would interrupt the situation in this way. Still he asked her, "What is it you want?"

She replied, "Please give us permission to pray to our God."

At that point Chaudhry said he was really irritated, but he said to her, "Well, go ahead but make it quick."

She immediately knelt down between her parents and the captain and began to pray aloud. He told me that at that point a flame of fire leaped out of the ground and blocked the family off completely from his sight. When I asked,

"Do you mean a literal flame of fire?" he replied, "A literal flame of fire! I could not even see them as long as she prayed." When she ceased praying, the fire receded into the ground. He did not kill them. He was so frightened that he immediately turned and ran.

At that point, Chaudhry said, he began to ask himself, "Who in the world is this God of the Christians? What kind of power does He have to do a thing like that?" This began a long search which lasted for a couple of years as he sought the truth about Jesus Christ. He was finally able to find the message of salvation and gave himself to Christ. At the time of his baptism as a new Christian he changed his name and called himself Ghulam Masih Naaman.

He told me that the reason for his name change was because Ghulam Masih in his language means "Servant of Messiah". "Naaman" is the name of a leper in the Old Testament who was healed from his leprosy by the prophet Elisha. Ghulam Masih Naaman wanted to be known as a servant of Messiah but he never wanted to forget that he also had been a spiritual leper. He was healed of his spiritual leprosy by Jesus Christ, so he added the name Naaman as a constant reminder of his former spiritual leprosy.

I was impressed by the straightforward power of God in the life of a man who was an enemy of the true God. God by His power turned this man's life around. Today he is an evangelist who travels all over Pakistan. He is fluent in several of the Pakistani dialects and preaches to people in their own language.

This to me is a powerful example of the power of prayer, the faith of a child and the working of the Holy Spirit in ways so much greater than most of us think possible. I have seen that power exhibited in many ways during my years growing up, my time as a missionary in Latin America and my worldwide opportunities to see God at work when I served as Director of World Evangelical Fellowship.

Many of those stories and experiences from my life are presented in the following pages.

SECTION ONE
Early Observations

CHAPTER ONE
The Day I Met George

"Do you want me to show you where the boys' restroom is?"

That single sentence from one eight-year-old boy to another had a profound influence on me and gave me the greatest possible lift at a time of desperate loneliness.

I was born in Germantown, Pennsylvania, part of the city of Philadelphia, and lived there until I was eight years old. Then my parents decided to move across the Delaware River to Moorestown, a small town in New Jersey just a few miles from Philadelphia. Their decision was absolutely traumatic to me. All my friends, all my contacts and all that was familiar to me were centered in Germantown. I loved my home, my friends, my school, my neighborhood, my church. The very thought of leaving all of this was devastating to me.

My older brother, Phil, and I were part of a neighborhood bunch of boys who were our friends. We played games together and most of us had "sled wagons" which were the same as snow sleds except that they had wheels and could be used on the sidewalks and streets year around. We would careen down the streets in a chain, hooked together with our feet in the bumper of the one behind us. It was great fun.

We also had snow sleds. There was a marvelous hill nearby in Fairmount Park called Thomas's Hill. We called it "Tommy's Hill." We could speed down one steep slope, up an adjacent slope, then down again beside a small stream. Then we would climb back up to the starting point and sled down again. We played hide and seek in the neighborhood, pulled pranks on each other and on some of our neighbors.

When our parents informed us about the proposed move to Moorestown, New Jersey, I was emotionally demolished. I began to pray ardently that this move would not go through. I asked my father what would happen if someone didn't buy our house in Germantown. He said, "Then we could not move to Moorestown." That was the spark that gave me hope. So I began to pray feverishly that the house would not sell. But it did, to my utter dismay.

I can still remember moving day vividly. The big truck pulled up and was loaded by the movers, and we drove away from that beloved house on Washington Lane. We headed across the Delaware River Bridge, now called the Benjamin Franklin Bridge, to our new home in Moorestown. I watched with sadness as the movers unloaded the household goods and set things up in our new house on Oak Avenue.

This was September 1936, and the school year was about to begin. So on the first day of school I walked to the local public school in abject loneliness. I did not know one person in town or in the school; I felt like crying the whole way to school. I was seated among the other fourth graders at a desk in the front row because I was short and the taller students were placed by size in the rows farther back.

When it came time for recess, we were lined up by size in front of the classroom before going out to the restrooms or the playground. Again I was in terrible fear because I had no idea what would take place. I had no friend at all.

Then the boy next to me in line, George Smith, spoke to me. The very idea that someone would even speak to me was startling. In a kindly way he asked, "Do you want me to show you where the boys' restroom is?" I could hardly contain both my surprise and my joy. Here was one boy who apparently was willing to be kind to me. That short word on his part, which he probably thought nothing of, was almost life changing for me, a lonely eight-year-old boy who thought his world had fallen apart.

George befriended me in other ways as well, and we became instant friends. He introduced me to other boys, explained things about Moorestown where he had lived all his life and made me feel that I belonged there. My nights of crying myself to sleep were soon gone; I was becoming a part of a new life.

As the years went on, George and I continued to be the best of friends. We even seemed to end up liking the same girls. In junior high school there was one gorgeous girl named Joyce. George and I fell desperately in "puppy love" with her. But George won out. Joyce was not remotely interested in me and made that abundantly clear in her stinging rejection of me. She really liked George. So much for my puppy love!

Then in high school the tables were turned. George and I both liked the same girl during our senior year. Somehow I seemed to win out on that one. She was a fine girl who had grown up in Africa of missionary parents. When

George graduated, he joined the navy just as World War II was winding down. I went to Wheaton College and met Phyllis, who would become my wife. Then my interest in high school friends waned rapidly.

Over the years George and I remained friends even though we didn't see much of each other after Phyllis and I went to the mission field. Then, in the age of computers and web sites, George found my name and address. We renewed our acquaintance after more than forty years. A few months before my beloved Phyllis died we were able to visit George and his wife, Alice, in Moorestown, where he had stayed for most of his adult life.

It was like old times as he and I drove around town reminiscing about our childhood and growing-up years. We went to see one of our old elementary school chums and enjoyed revisiting our old haunts. Having spent much of his life there, George was able to update me on town developments.

It is amazing to me how one question that George spoke to me on that first day of school, indicating friendship, could almost revolutionize my emotional state. I have long since realized that my fears and sadness back then were unnecessary, but at the time those fears represented my entire world.

The example that George set for me in reaching out to a desperately lonely little boy has been an undergirding challenge to me all of my life. I thank the Lord for George and for what he did for me, even though at the time George probably hardly thought of it as anything significant. I am reminded of that day many times when I realize that perhaps I should be reaching out to a lonely person who might be encouraged by some small step of friendship that I could take. May God help me to respond to such opportunities when they come along.

CHAPTER TWO
A Young Patriot

———

"The Japanese have just bombed Pearl Harbor!" My father announced this to our family on Sunday afternoon, December 7, 1941 with a sense of urgency in his voice. I had never heard of Pearl Harbor so had no idea where it was nor of the implications. It was not long, of course, before it became clear to all of us what was going on. I learned where Pearl Harbor is, what was located there and why the Japanese had bombed it.

The next day in school we sat transfixed in class as the teacher had us listen by radio to President Roosevelt's famous speech to Congress in which he referred to December 7 as "a date which will live in infamy." He went on to ask Congress for permission to declare a state of war against the Empire of Japan. A declaration of war with the two other Axis countries, Germany and Italy, followed. We were plunged into the greatest, most extensive and most devastating war in history.

I was thirteen years old at the time so there was no thought of joining the military forces. However, the profound patriotism that swept the country rubbed off thoroughly on me. I learned the patriotic songs of the day such as, "Let's Remember Pearl Harbor," along with many old songs from World War I that were immediately resurrected. These included such favorites as, "Over There," "Johnny, Get Your Gun" and many others.

We heard the calls to buy war bonds to help finance the war. We saw billboards filled with such calls and patriotic slogans. We saw pictures of the men and women lining up to enlist to serve the country. As a young boy I had always been fascinated with uniforms but never had the opportunity to wear one. I loved seeing Marines in their immaculate dress blues, nurses in their starched white outfits, airmen with their wings on their chests, infantrymen in their khakis, sailors in their bell-bottomed trousers.

There were also warnings on behalf of the Coast Guardsmen who had to transport the men and materiel overseas. We were warned not to give out any information that might jeopardize their safety. One telling poster showed a wide-open sea with one sailor's cap floating alone on the surface and the stark words, "Somebody blabbed."

German submarines were soon roaming the Atlantic and causing havoc with our shipping. Dozens of ships were going down every month. Some of these were just off the east coast of the U.S. I recall going down to the New Jersey beaches to see the stern of a sunken merchant ship sticking up out of the water just a few miles from the beach. It was a grim reminder of the war, even though our shores never suffered what Europe and Asia went through.

I saw the USO centers where servicemen and women were welcomed for coffee and doughnuts and many other services at any time of the day or night. People got up and gave their seats on the train to men and women in uniform.

We had to get monthly ration cards to buy our limited quota of gasoline. This was also true for our meat, eggs and butter, automobile tires and other goods that were essential for serving the war movement. But complaints were few and far between. The entire atmosphere of the country was one of unity to support the effort to defeat the enemy that had been thrust unexpectedly upon us.

Conscientious Objectors (known as "C.O.s") who refused to carry a gun for religious or other reasons were sometimes ostracized and, unfortunately, looked down upon. Many of them ended up in auxiliary services such as the medical corps or went into civilian wartime duty. Some ended up in C.O. camps for the duration.

In the midst of this stirring atmosphere I tried to do my part. I had enjoyed reading a series of books for boys with titles such as *A Patriot Lad in Old New Hampshire* and *A Patriot Lad of Old Philadelphia* and similar stories from the Revolutionary War. So I decided that since I was not old enough to enlist, I would do what I could to make my small contribution to the war effort. I had a newspaper route in which I delivered the *Philadelphia Evening Bulletin* and always read the headlines and front pages as I was folding the papers for delivery. So I kept up on the progress of the war.

There were several specific areas where I could make my contribution. I saved up enough money from my paper route to buy a $25 war bond, which I later redeemed with some accumulated interest after the war. I helped to collect scrap metal by rummaging through our garage and attic to find any old metal that could be turned in to produce war materiel. I scouted the neighborhood to collect anything that might be called scrap metal. I once even got free entrance into a football game between the University of Pennsylvania and Penn State because the university offered free admission to anyone who brought in ten pounds of scrap metal. I was thrilled and proud to do so.

We also had a victory garden. The government encouraged us to plant victory gardens where we would grow our own vegetables and thus alleviate pressure on our farmers who were producing great quantities of food for the armed forces. I plowed up a section of our backyard and planted such things as tomatoes, corn, beans, spinach, carrots, radishes and other vegetables. I bought a cultivator to use in keeping down the weeds between the rows of plants. It always pleased me when my mother used my produce to feed our family.

The climax of my wartime efforts came when I joined "The Ground Observer Corps." At the beginning of the war the U.S. had not yet perfected radar, although it was rapidly being developed. There was some fear that Germany might try suicide bombings on our east coast in places such as Boston, New York, Philadelphia and Washington D.C. Germany did not have planes that could fly across the Atlantic and still return to Germany. But the feeling was that they might try to fly across, bomb our cities and not worry about the fate of their planes.

Therefore the Army Air Corps (the Air Corps was not yet a separate entity) developed a series of spotter posts along the entire east coast from Maine to Florida. They built towers on high ground with telephone links to central locations. The towers were close enough together so that planes in any part of the sky along the coast could be spotted by the people in a tower. When a plane left the area where an observer in one area could spot it, an observer in another tower could pick up the progress.

The Army Air Corps then trained civilian volunteers to man these spotter towers. My father and I volunteered. We were then given intensive training by the Army Air Corps in how to recognize all the planes, commercial and military, that were in use at that time. We learned how to identify the planes from every angle. We could tell a British Spitfire, a German Stukka, even a Japanese Zero, although there was no possibility that Japanese planes could reach our east coast. We knew all the American planes by sight, the B-17, B-24, B-25, P-40, P-47, P-51 and all the others. We could also tell the commercial planes such as the old faithful DC-3 and the smaller planes.

After we successfully completed our training, we were assigned to a tower and given a weekly time slot when we would spend four hours in that tower.

The closest tower to Moorestown, where we lived, was just a few miles outside of town on the only little hill in that flat country. It was a crossroads of a small farming village and was named Mt. Laurel.

Every Saturday my father and I went out to that tower on Mt. Laurel and did our duty as plane spotters. Our job was to watch and listen for planes in our area. If we could see the plane, we would immediately call the regional center, identify the plane and tell the direction in which it was flying. If it was cloudy and we could only hear the plane, we tried to determine the direction in which it was flying and call to give that information. If we could see it but could not fully identify the plane, we still called in and gave all the information possible.

With this system, the entire east coast was covered day and night with civilian volunteers who were in the chain of towers delivering information to the Army Air Corps, which was ready, if necessary, to send up fighters immediately if the plane was suspected of being an enemy plane.

I enjoyed my four-hour watch every week. My father used the time in the tower to talk with me about some of the issues of life that a teenager should begin thinking about. He gave me some valuable insights into life in general and into the slippery slopes of adolescent years. I look back on those times with deep thankfulness for a father who took that sort of interest in his son and who used those times in the tower to teach me.

Within a year of the outbreak of World War II the U.S. had perfected radar, so The Ground Observer Corps was disbanded. But I kept the official certificate awarded to me by the Unites States Army Air Corps as having successfully completed their training. I was proud that I had been able to serve my country in a limited way with the activities that a young teenager could carry out.

Toward the end of the war I received my call for duty and reported for medical exams. I was given the date when I should report for duty. But before that date arrived, the war ended and President Truman called a draft holiday. So I was never inducted.

I shall always look back on those years with thankfulness for what I learned as I watched the progress of the war, the unifying of our country and the opportunity to serve in the small way that I could contribute.

As I think back on the lessons learned during that period of my life, I am impressed with the similarities to my mission work spanning over half a century. As a "young patriot" I knew I was on the right side. My government had no choice but to respond to the unprovoked attacks launched against us. When my president called for help from all age groups, I responded in the best way I could. The mobilization of the country required total commitment.

When my Master called for His followers to tell the story of His love and grace to the whole world, I had no choice but to respond. In World War II I could respond only in a limited way because of my age. But I did the best I could. In God's army for missions, I could respond with total commitment.

That call meant different things to different people. During WW II, we were told that for every soldier on the front lines there were eleven people in support services behind the lines. In the call to missions, I felt God wanted me on the front lines, and I responded accordingly. Yet I have been deeply thankful for all those behind the lines who have made the long-term mission service possible.

During my college years right after World War II, two things became clear to me. First, the Master commands us to give the gospel to the whole world. Second, the parts of the world that had the least opportunity to hear the gospel were not in my own country. Most of the inhabitants of my country could hear the gospel if they so desired. Churches were in every town. There were bookstores with Bibles, radio and TV programs, and gospel preaching everywhere. This meant that most of my country could hear the good news. But vast areas of the world did not have this opportunity.

Having responded as a boy to the President's call during World War II, I did not find it hard to respond to the Master's call, with total commitment to the Lord Jesus Christ to go into the world with His message.

CHAPTER THREE
The Yum Yum Lady

She was a wrinkled little elderly lady with a charming smile and a sweet, friendly spirit. She was also an African-American who in those days was known as a "colored person." She lived just one block from our home in Germantown, Pennsylvania. In those days our society was segregated. We never played with the African-American boys even though they lived near us. They went to one school and we went to another.

Nevertheless, in the summer, we went around the corner to visit the "Yum Yum Lady." We were at the height of the Great Depression in the early and middle 1930s. Most people had to do what they could to eke out a living. I don't remember this lady's name but I can see her very clearly in my mind. In the heat of summer she produced what we called "Yum Yums." They were little paper cups filled with crushed ice that was colored with some sugar water. She had three sizes, a small nut cup for one penny, a slightly larger nut cup for two pennies and a Dixie-cup size for five pennies.

Because my family was also scraping to make ends meet, it was not a daily occurrence for us children to be able to buy even the smallest yum yum. But several times during the summer my mother would give single pennies to Phil, Betty and me to get yum yum cups. Once in a while, if we begged hard enough, she might give us two pennies each. But never once did we experience a five-cent Dixie cup size. That was beyond what Mother could give us.

It was a great treat to go around the corner to the Yum Yum Lady for those cups of colored ice. But part of the treat was her marvelous smile and her cheerful greeting. We always had a few minutes to chat with her. She was always so friendly and kind to anyone who came to her home. As I reflect on her, I am amazed to realize that we children feared the children who lived in her neighborhood.

A few years later, my family moved across the Delaware River to Moorestown, New Jersey, and when I was twelve years old I was able to get a paper route. I had about fifty customers. Part of my route went through the African-American neighborhood. On collection day every two weeks, I had to collect thirty-six cents from each customer. The paper cost three cents a day for six days a week. I received one cent per paper.

One of my customers in the African-American neighborhood was a Mrs. Yancey. She reminded me of the Yum Yum Lady. She had an equally charming smile and a gracious spirit. When collection day came she was always prepared to give me not only the thirty-six cents but delicious warm, fresh-baked cookies. Again, I look back and wonder how I could ever have had fearful thoughts about someone of her color.

In our town there were four football teams which, in today's jargon, might be called "Little League." These were not leagues as such but just four teams made up of boys who loved to play. I played on a team called "The Stanwick Braves" even though I could never claim to be any great star as a football player.

One of the teams was "The Tigers." This team was composed totally of African-Americans. The other three teams were white. The Tigers always mopped up the other teams. They were far superior to us in their athletic ability, and playing against them I found that my ungrounded fear of them began to dissipate. One time I told an adult friend that I was playing that day against "The Tigers." He responded, "You are playing with them? I would never let one of them put his hands on me." I was shocked by what he said but it made me realize the depth of feeling that some white people had against their neighbors.

I don't know how long it took me to get beyond the segregated mind-set that held so many of us in those days. I am ashamed to think that it even existed, and I would like to believe that it finally disappeared from my heart and mind. Years later, when we lived in Latin America, we taught our own small children that delightful little chorus:

Jesus loves the little children, all the children of the world.
Red and yellow, black and white, they are precious in His sight;
Jesus loves the little children of the world.

One day, when singing this song with our son David Jr., who may have been about four or five at the time, he turned to me with a puzzled look and asked, "Daddy, what is a black child?" I replied, "Well, your good friend Carlitos is black."

He still looked puzzled as he meditated on this. The idea that some of his friends were a different color hadn't occurred to him. This was a great contrast to my outlook on people at his age. Many of my children's friends were various shades of darker colors but it didn't matter to them.

I'd like to believe that my thinking has been cleansed of prejudice. But I am aware that "the heart is deceitful above all things, and desperately wicked" (Jeremiah 17:9 KJV). And I know that my wicked heart may still deceive me in this area. However, I am thankful that the Lord has dealt mercifully with me as I have tried to learn lessons from those of other races. I am sure that I am still in the learning process, but I hope that I am learning well.

CHAPTER FOUR
My Father's Hands

The photo is an old snapshot. It shows my father as a young man, probably about 19 or 20 years old, holding himself out in midair from a parallel bar. The remarkable thing is that this is not a picture of chinning himself up; rather, the bar is behind his back and he is holding his body out suspended in the air. I used to marvel at seeing this picture, realizing how strong those hands and arms had to be to produce such a position.

My father's hands were exceptionally strong. As a young boy, I used to enjoy watching those hands in a wide variety of activities. I heard that he used to take a Philadelphia telephone book and tear it in two with his hands. I never saw him do this, as it was done only in his younger years. But his parents and his sisters confirmed to me that he actually did this. He could also take a ten-penny spike and bend it with his hands. I have seen him do that.

He used to play the piano with firmness and gusto. He was not a great piano player by any stretch of the imagination, but the strength of his touch on the keys made the music unmistakably clear and easy to follow. He often played the piano for our Sunday school at church. Everyone knew, without question, what the tune was.

He also played for us at home. As small children we loved to march around the living room as he played martial-like music. He even composed one small ditty himself and used to play it so that we would march with firm determination. He called it "The Burlington County March," taking the name of the county in New Jersey where we lived.

My father loved outdoor work in our yard and would chop wood with great pleasure. Those strong hands were perfectly suited to such work. They also helped him with one of his favorite hobbies, which was fly-fishing for trout. He grasped the fly rod firmly and cast a long smooth line.

When we spent time in the summer in New Hampshire, Dad taught us children about the flowers, the trees, the birds, and took us on bird hikes. He taught us how to climb the forested mountains which rose above the timberline. He also taught us the art of fly-fishing.

When he was in college, first in Haverford College and then the University of Pennsylvania where he graduated, he enjoyed wrestling. However, because he had lost one eye in a Fourth of July accident as a twelve-year-old boy, the doctor told him not to wrestle. The possibility of an injury to his remaining eye was not worth the risk. So he only wrestled for fun, not for the team. But he once told me that he remembered one companion who refused to wrestle with him even for fun. The friend said, "It's those hands of yours. I can't compete with such strong hands."

Dad loved to play magic tricks with children. One of his favorites involved those large hands. He would take a small penknife, show it to the children and then supposedly swallow it. In the process he would drop it down at his feet, pick it up and feign swallowing it again. But with the knife concealed in those large hands, he would slip it behind his knee (he always sat down to do this trick). Then opening his mouth and his hands wide, he would show the children that the knife was gone. Then with a deft movement he would "find" the knife behind the collar of one of the children standing by. Kids always loved this and seldom figured out how he did it.

He had another little routine in which he would rapidly slap his fingers loudly and in rhythm off his knees and off the back of his hands, making a loud rhythmic drumming that sounded almost like music. We used to love watching him do this.

Did we ever feel the force of those hands on our little posteriors? Yes, we did. He and our mother believed in the biblical admonitions such as: "He who spares the rod hates his son, but he who loves him is careful to discipline him" (Proverbs 13:24 NIV). And, "Folly is bound up in the heart of a child, but the rod of discipline will drive it far from him" (Proverbs 22:15 NIV). And, "The rod of correction imparts wisdom, but a child left to himself disgraces his mother" (Proverbs 29:15 NIV). And, "Discipline your son, and he will give you peace; he will bring delight to your soul" (Proverbs 29:17 NIV).

My father never used a rod or belt when he punished us, but that big hand was quite sufficient. He never abused us, and his discipline was always done in understanding love. But I dreaded that hand. If I disobeyed during the day, when Father was not at home, and the disobedience was of special seriousness, the worst thing Mother could do was to postpone discipline and say that this will wait until Daddy comes home. I would beg her to get it over with now, as Daddy's hand was dreaded far more than her hairbrush. But one thing was always clear. There would be a loving explanation for the punishment before it was delivered. And it was always done in such a way that we understood that he loved us. It was never harsh or abusive, but it was supremely effective partly because of the size and strength in his hands.

And those hands were also used in loving ways. In my early years, when we were still living in Germantown, my mother would allow me to go up the street to wait for Daddy in the late afternoon. He would be coming up the hill from the train station, having commuted from downtown Philadelphia. I would wait to see his head bobbing up and down through the crowd of commuters. He was six feet three inches tall, so his head could be seen above the other commuters. Then I would dash to greet him. He would catch me up in his arms, with those big hands grabbing me and holding me close in greeting. I loved those times and was thankful for such hands.

At bedtime he would come into my bedroom, sit down on the bed beside me, stroke my brow with those loving hands, then pray with me. Again, those were memorable times for which I am thankful to this day. I had a father who loved me, disciplined me and gave me a settled sense of security. Those strong hands formed a wonderful basis for such loving security.

As I raised my own four children I tried to follow the example set by my father. I believe the exhortations from the book of Proverbs about proper discipline of children. I tried to avoid overly harsh discipline, and I never used a belt or switch. But as my father did with me, I used my hand on posterior parts as needed. I hope my children understood that I loved them and that these hands, properly used, demonstrated that love.

Apparently I inherited some of my father's strength of hand, although I never could tear a large telephone book in half or bend a ten-penny spike. As a college wrestler I was occasionally told that my strong hands were especially beneficial in that sport.

On the mission field there were times when strength of hand was taxed to the limit. When trudging through the jungles with a backpack, I sometimes had to carry additional baggage such as my cornet case and an extra zipper bag or a box of books. While each one individually was not overly heavy, by the end of a long day of traversing muddy trails, climbing high mountain ridges or other difficult terrain, the extra items carried by hand felt like lead weight. At such times I was thankful for the strong hands that my father had passed on to me.

CHAPTER FIVE
Grandpa Howard and Me

"Dave, would you be so kind as to read something from the Bible to me this afternoon?"

My grandfather, Philip E. Howard Sr., and I were sitting on the veranda of his summer place in the White Mountains of New Hampshire. Gale Cottage had been built around 1886 by an uncle (by marriage) of the Howard family and had been passed on to my grandfather, who later passed it on to his children and subsequently to the ensuing generations. (It is still in our family, owned by a niece of mine.) We were looking out directly at the Franconia Range of the White Mountains, with Mt. Lafayette, Cannon Mountain, Bald Mountain, Eagle Cliff and Mt. Kinsman all in full view.

However, it is inaccurate to say that "we" were seeing that range. Grandpa Howard was nearly blind as he neared the end of his life. So he could not see the beautiful view that I could see, which is why he was asking me to read to him. I was there at Gale Cottage for part of the summer to help make his time more enjoyable. I would chop wood, build fires in the massive fireplace in the spacious parlor, help him in and out of the car when we went on outings and in general be available for any and all tasks that would be of help to an elderly man who was limited physically. I was fifteen years old.

"Yes, Grandpa, of course I will be glad to read to you. What would you like me to read?"

"Read the first chapter of Revelation." So I gladly complied and read chapter one.

"Read the next chapter," he said, which I did. "And the next," and on it went. Before I knew it, I had read aloud through the entire book of Revelation. As I got to the last chapters of that great book, where descriptions of heaven and the final triumph of the Lord in history burst out with glorious and triumphant exclamations and hallelujahs, I saw that Grandpa was sobbing. Tears were pouring down his wrinkled cheeks. He knew he was getting close to those marvelous scenes.

His beloved wife of well over fifty years, my Grandma Howard, was already in heaven waiting for him, as she had gone on to glory the previous year. His love for her was deep and very evident. More than that, his love for the Lord and his desire to see the Lord face to face was uppermost in his mind.

For a fifteen-year-old boy to read aloud, without stopping, the entire book of Revelation, and to see an elderly, godly man reacting as Grandpa reacted to those marvelous descriptions of the triumph of God, made a deep and lasting impression on me. To the end of my life, I will cherish that memory as one of the significant moments of my early life.

When Grandpa Howard died, six outstanding Christian men, all of whom were leaders of the evangelical movement of that day, were asked to be pallbearers at his funeral. Later those men told my father that in the car driving to the cemetery they shared their thoughts about Grandpa Howard. He was the publisher of the *Sunday School Times*, which was possibly the leading Christian journal of that day. They all agreed that he was the most Christ-like man they had ever known. His loving, gracious spirit, his concern for other people, his unbelievably kind way of dealing with people and his deeply evident love for the Lord permeated all that he was and did.

I look back today, and that scene on the veranda of Gale Cottage is one of the most precious memories of a childhood filled with the blessings of growing up in a godly family.

Today I have thirteen grandchildren. Because of geographical distances, I do not see them nearly as often as I saw my own Grandpa Howard. I do wonder if my life and example to them will be as vivid and as happy as mine is for my grandfather. His quiet love for people, his unswerving integrity in his professional life, his dedication to his family, including his grandchildren, his spontaneous laugh as he enjoyed good humor, his love for the Lord and for His Word all combined to produce a person as close to a true saint as I have ever known.

A few years ago, I was expressing deep-seated anger about a person who had harmed our daughter over a period of many years. My daughter, however, had forgiven this person and she wanted me to do likewise. As she exhorted me to forgive that person, she said, "Dad, I don't want you to die a bitter old man. I want you to be a happy old man who shows love for others and is Christ-like in life just like your Grandpa Howard."

This was a sobering challenge to me, especially as it was placed in the context of Grandpa Howard. After some deep struggle, I believe I was able to forgive that person who had harmed our daughter so badly. I am thankful for the example she used to remind me of Grandpa.

The apostle Paul, probably the greatest missionary of all time, said to the Corinthian believers, "Be ye followers of me, even as I also am of Christ" (1 Corinthians 11:1 KJV). I tried to do that in my life as a missionary.

Today, even though I am myself a grandfather and no longer on a foreign mission field, I still want to be a follower of my Grandpa Howard even as he was a follower of Christ.

CHAPTER SIX
A Tale of Two Spinsters

"Spinster—an elderly woman who has not married; old maid" (World Book Dictionary).

That generally accepted definition of the word "spinster" carries a negative connotation in most contexts. It is sometimes used to mock or belittle a woman. However, the dictionary also gives another definition as follows: "a woman who spins flax, wool or the like, into thread."

That woman takes her creative abilities plus material at her disposal and puts them together to produce something valuable and useful. There were two such "spinsters" who influenced my life for the good.

My father had two sisters who never married. The older of the two, Alice, graduated from Wheaton College and Yale School of Nursing. She became an effective and unusually gifted nurse. For many years she was the "Visiting Nurse" to her home community as well as being head nurse in several different hospitals.

When World War II broke out, Alice enlisted in the U.S. Army Nursing Corps and went overseas where she spent the war years caring for wounded soldiers who were sent back from the European front to England for recuperation. She rose rapidly in the ranks because of her leadership abilities. By the end of the war she was a major, which was an exceptionally high rank for a woman in those days.

On one occasion in London, she was invited to report for a "secret operation" with a small group of high-ranking U.S. military officers. She had no idea what the purpose was nor where they were going. When the group of specially selected officers was gathered, they were taken in a vehicle to an unknown destination. Upon arrival, they realized that they were at Buckingham Palace. They had been selected for a private reception with

King George VI and Queen Elizabeth. The two young princesses, Elizabeth (now the Queen) and Margaret Rose, were also present. Thus the qualities of leadership and character, which were evident in Alice's life, were the reason for this invitation.

The younger sister, Anne, also graduated from Wheaton College. But instead of entering a profession, she returned home to care lovingly for her elderly parents who needed special attention. Up until the death of both parents, which took place in 1943 and 1946, her major work was ministering to them, although she did a few other jobs at certain periods.

Her abilities opened up several significant positions for her at different times. For some years she served as personal secretary to Dr. Frank E. Gaebelein, founder and headmaster of The Stony Brook School, an ivy league Christian prep school on Long Island. Dr.Gaebelein was also a highly respected biblical scholar and author. When she worked as his secretary, Anne often typed his manuscripts.

Later she also served as personal secretary to the president of National Bible Institute in New York City, Dr. J. Oliver Buswell. He had been president of Wheaton College when Anne was a student. He also was a world-renowned Bible scholar and theologian.

To me, as a young boy growing up in the suburbs of Philadelphia, they were "Aunt Alice" and "Aunt Anne." In later years they both insisted that my siblings and I drop the label "aunt" and address them by their first names. They were close friends to us.

When my birthday came around Anne would take me for a private dinner to a nice restaurant in Philadelphia where just the two of us would have time together. These were always special times for me.

When my younger sister, Virginia, was born, Alice came and stayed with us three older siblings while Mother was in the hospital. The day Virginia was born, February 7, was the coldest day in the history of Philadelphia. As a rather energetic six year old, I managed that day to break the window in my bedroom, which was the only really warm room in our old three-story home. Alice took this in stride; she never rebuked me for my foolish carelessness, but rather hung up a rug over the window to try to hold some heat inside until my father came home and could repair the window.

Summers, when we went to Gale Cottage, Alice and Anne often came too, spending time with us there. Anne was especially gifted in knowing the flowers. She and my sister Elisabeth (who later became well known as Elisabeth Elliot, widow of martyred missionary Jim Elliot) were kindred spirits in this area.

Elisabeth has often written in her best-selling books about Gale Cottage and what she learned there.

One summer, at our home in Moorestown, Alice announced to me that she was going to the cottage the next week. Then she added, on the spur of the moment, "Would you like to go with me? Come on, let's go." So I joined her on the train trip to New Hampshire. Anne was already there caring for my grandparents.

One day, Alice and Anne planned a special hike for me up Mt. Lafayette, the highest mountain in the Franconia Range. I was twelve years old and this was a thrilling outing for me. We started in the midafternoon and hiked part way up to the Greenleaf Hut, a way station on the Appalachian Trail that runs from Maine to Georgia. It is a rustic mountain hut manned in the summer by college students, known as "hut masters," who serve the hikers.

That evening we had a delicious dinner prepared and served by the hut masters. Then we hiked over to a nearby lookout and watched the most magnificent sunset I had ever seen out over the rolling green hills to the west. It was so beautiful that my heart felt a deep longing which I could not define for myself but which undoubtedly was an appreciation of the majestic beauty given to us by our Creator. We sang the doxology together as the sun sank below the distant hills.

The next morning the hut masters woke us up at 3:00 a.m. Taking blankets for the crisp, cold mountain air, they guided us up the rest of the mountain to the peak of Mt. Lafayette. Off to the east lies the Presidential Range including Mt. Washington, the second highest peak east of the Mississippi. We wrapped ourselves in the blankets and lay on the rocks to watch the sunrise over Mt. Washington. I am not a sufficient enough wordsmith to describe the overpowering beauty of that sunrise. It was without question the most magnificent I had ever seen, before or since.

At one point the words of a favorite gospel hymn came to my mind. I have never sung this song since that day without remembering that unique youthful experience.

"I'm pressing on the upward way, new heights I'm gaining ev'ry day—still praying as I'm onward bound, 'Lord, plant my feet on higher ground.'

"I want to scale the utmost heights and catch a gleam of glory bright; but still I'll pray till heaven I've found, 'Lord lead me on to higher ground.'"

After the sun had risen and the sky was brilliant in the sparkling mountain air, we descended to the Greenleaf Hut where we were served a bountiful mountain breakfast. Later in the morning we wound our way down the mountain trail and returned to Gale Cottage. The memory of that trip with the indescribable sunset and sunrise is indelibly etched on my mind. But I am also heavily indebted to and thankful for those two "spinster" aunts who loved and cared for a young nephew and wanted to give him an unforgettable experience.

As I reflect on how these two aunts wove such memories into the threads of my life, I am reminded of many other single women I have known over the years. As one whose entire life has been involved in mission, I have seen the remarkable influence that single women have had in the spread of the gospel.

When my sister, Elisabeth Elliot, lost her husband, Jim Elliot, to the spears of the Waodani Indians in Ecuador, she continued on for many years as a single woman before remarrying. One outstanding mission leader said to me some years later, "Your sister Elisabeth, in my mind, has been the most influential woman in missions in the entire latter half of the twentieth century." Over the years I have met scores—maybe hundreds—of people who have told me, with deep sincerity, that Elisabeth's life in speaking and writing has profoundly influenced their walk with the Lord and their involvement in missions.

I also think of a colleague in Colombia whom my children called "Aunt Jean." She arrived in Colombia in 1957, took up a position in an evangelical school and never went anywhere else for more than 50 years. When she finally retired she left her mark on the lives of hundreds of students who loved her as "Miss Jean." For years she cared for the school principal whose health gave out and who needed personal care. Her length of uninterrupted service must be some sort of record for staying faithfully in one position for more than half a century.

A missionary nurse came into our home when Phyllis gave birth to our fourth child by caesarean section. Because of the major operation, Phyllis was not able to care adequately for our three other children during her recuperation. This single nurse took over household duties and cared lovingly for our small children. Over the years she still keeps in touch with our family, following with real interest the developments of our children.

Missionary biographies and mission history are full of stories of the godly single women who have been true pioneers and leaders in spreading the gospel. In my extensive travels around the world, it has been exciting to see the powerful influence that single women have had in so many places. The worldwide church of Jesus Christ owes a deep debt of gratitude to these women whose vision and dedication have been in the vanguard of mission advance. They deserve our gratitude and praise.

CHAPTER SEVEN

The Pleasure of Hard Work

Hard work never did me (or most other boys, for that matter) any harm. Growing up during the Great Depression of the 1930s, I was aware that money did not grow on trees and that if I needed money it was primarily my responsibility to work for it. While my parents did provide a small allowance during some of my growing-up years, it was minimal and was not always available. So I looked forward to the time when I could earn some money for myself.

My eyes were set on getting a newspaper delivery route. The newspapers of that time required that a boy must be twelve years old. So that was my target age. When I reached that age, I was able to deliver the *Philadelphia Evening Bulletin*, which has long since gone out of existence.

Each day a truck from the *Evening Bulletin* delivered to a loading platform in our town a stack of newspapers bound in wire or rope, according to each route to be delivered. We delivery boys would each take our stack of papers, fold them with a special fold that allowed us to throw the paper onto the porch and place them in a large canvas bag that we carried over our shoulders. My route had fifty-two homes on half a dozen streets.

Collection day was every two weeks on Friday. The paper cost three cents a day. I would collect 36 cents for the six-day, two-week period. This meant ringing the doorbell of each house to collect the cash. I earned one cent for each paper and would send two cents per paper to the newspaper company. Thus I was able to earn $6.24 every two weeks. That was a good early work experience for me.

Another early experience came in the offices of the *Sunday School Times*, the weekly evangelical newspaper whose editor was my father. The paper was printed in the basement of their office building on a huge ancient press that must have dated to the 19th century. During school breaks and several times in the summer

I was employed there either as an office boy to run errands or as a helper in the pressroom.

I also mowed lawns in our neighborhood. I offered to mow the lawns of a number of neighbors who were glad to pay 35 cents an hour to an ambitious boy. One summer I had nearly every home in one block around our home. I had an old push mower and leaned how to sharpen the blades myself. I was proud of my work and appreciated seeing the results of my efforts as I surveyed each recently mowed lawn.

One summer I worked at the Quaker cemetery near my home. This meant not only mowing the grass but also clipping by hand around every one of the small gravestones. By the time I finished using a hand clipper around every stone my hand was blistered and sore. The responsibilities given to me in those jobs were good training for me in later life.

While we did not live on a farm, I had the opportunity of working on several different farms during my teenage years and early 20s. Each summer, when our family went to Gale Cottage, I worked at a small farm across the field from the cottage. The owner, Jamie Smith, had a few cows, a couple of horses, a pen of pigs and some chickens. He produced his own hay and feed and also grew vegetables.

Even as a small boy I enjoyed joining him on his hay wagon or hay rake as he brought in the hay for his animals. Watching him milk the cows and feed the chickens was a daily routine. Watching his wife using the separator to skim the milk to get the thick cream was another enjoyable pastime. When I was old enough I pitched hay with him even though I was not working for pay. I also learned how to harness and drive the horses.

But a few miles up the road was a beautiful farm known as "Profile Farm," situated on the lower slopes of Cannon Mountain. The farm took its name from the famous "Old Man of the Mountain" that was also known as "The Great Stone Face." One summer I worked at Profile Farm. I would ride my bike several miles to the farm and work all day with the tenant farmer. I learned how to use a large scythe to mow weeds as well as to harvest some crops such as millet. I pitched and stacked hay and weeded gardens and drove a team of horses.

The hardest work I ever did was on Gruno's Dairy Farm on the outskirts of Moorestown. The Grunos were a hard-working German family consisting of an elderly father and mother and four big, strong, thick-armed sons plus a couple of daughters. They worked steadily from sunup to sundown every day, including the elderly father who worked alongside his sons and kept up with them.

I would arrive on my bicycle at 7:00 a.m. and was never free to leave before 6:00 p.m., and sometimes later. One of the sons would give me my orders for the day in as few words as possible; then he would turn me loose. I was expected to do my job without further instructions.

The work was widely varied. Some days I would be cleaning out the cow stalls or the bull pen. They had one ferocious and dangerous bull. One day I was given instructions to clean out the bull pen. The bull was outside the pen in the corral. My job was to clean out the manure and pitch it out to a wheelbarrow. One day the son who gave me my orders added, "If dat bull gets in, you know what to do." I thought I knew, but just to be sure asked, "What?" He said, "Get out." That was enough said.

Other days I would work behind a team of horses cultivating the rows of newly sprouting corn or a scratch harrow breaking up the hard ground between rows. Often I worked out in the hayfields hoisting hundred-pound bales of hay onto a truck to be taken into the barn for feed. This was the hardest work I had ever done in my life. I was in college then, and as a wrestler I thought I was in pretty good shape. But that job of tossing and stacking those bales of hay taxed every ounce of strength and energy I had.

The Gruno family worked hard and steadily together, and I was expected to keep up. My pay was fifty cents an hour, or five dollars a day. I actually spent eleven hours a day or more at the farm but, since we took one hour for lunch, I was paid for ten hours.

Since this was a dairy farm, I was told I could drink all the milk I wanted from the barn. Since I perspired freely in that hot summer sun out in the field, I usually drank milk instead of water to quench my thirst. By the end of the day I would have downed about a gallon of milk.

Even later on, as a missionary, I continued to do some of this kind of work while on furlough. My wife, Phyllis, came from a family of hard-working Montana ranchers. Both of her grandfathers had homesteaded in the hard soil of south-central Montana. Her father worked the ranch of his father-in-law until, in later years, he was able to purchase his own ranch. He raised sheep and wheat and hay for their feed. He always had a few cows and horses. On several occasions I was able to work with him.

During one of our furloughs we were in Montana during lambing season. This was in March, when the weather was still cold. Someone had to get up every two hours through the night to go out into the field and rescue the newly born lambs to get them into the barn so that they would not freeze to death. I worked with Phyllis's parents, spelling them off in two-hour shifts during the night. We had to go out into the cold, find the lambs, then get the ewe to follow into the barn so that she could suckle her lamb. If the ewe did not follow and was thus lost in the herd, the new lamb became a "bum lamb" that had to be fed by hand.

In the summer of 1952, our first son, David Jr., was born in Montana. We were heading for the mission field in a few months but I needed to earn some extra money as we prepared to go. So I got a job on the Northern Pacific Railroad. I worked with a team known as the "Gandy Dancers." These were men who straightened tracks by sheer physical effort. We worked side by side with crowbars under the direction of a foreman. He looked for the slight bends in the tracks that needed to be straightened. Under his direction the men would drive their crow bars in unison under the tracks and at his signal would give a hard heave to move the steel track back into its straight position. All day we heaved against the steel tracks as we worked our way along.

Working alongside men from totally different lifestyles, whose language and outlook on life was far removed from my background, was valuable for me in many ways. Each of the jobs contributed in some way to my personal growth. Learning how to work in a variety of settings had its benefits later on in my missionary work.

Straightening out hard steel rails on the Northern Pacific Railroad was an impossible task for one man working alone. It took a team of "Gandy Dancers" working in unison under the direction of a foreman who called out the orders. Missionary work often requires the same kind of teamwork, with everyone pulling together under the direction of the foreman who calls out the orders.

No one reading the *Sunday School Times* would ever think of a teenage boy and a couple of seasoned printers working in a dusty, humid basement beside an ancient printing press. But the journal itself brought blessing and helpful challenges to thousands of people. Much missionary work is often done "behind the scenes" with no public recognition. But it can be a channel of great blessing to many.

Some of my early work experiences were fun. I enjoyed mowing lawns and seeing the trim results. I loved pitching hay on an old wagon with a pitchfork and a team of horses. But clipping grass by hand around hundreds of small gravestones in a Quaker cemetery was not fun, and the resulting blisters, sore hands and aching knees were painful. But this had to be done if the cemetery was to look acceptable. In those days we had no power trimmers to do the work for us.

The same is also true in our missionary work. Some of it is great fun. I always enjoyed riding on a mule through the forests or up steep mountain ridges. I loved riding in dugout canoes up a jungle river and watching the beautiful bird life, the alligators basking in the sun on the riverbanks and the plush forest foliage or drifting quietly down river on a raft.

But there were always the hard unrewarding tasks which often left "blisters" on my heart and soul but which had to be done if the desired results were to be reached.

As I think back on over half a century of missionary work, one "blister" that stands out on my soul, almost more than any other, is about my friend Alvaro whom I tell about in detail in a later chapter. After two years of mentoring, discipling and training him, and watching him apparently grow in grace and in the knowledge of the Lord Jesus Christ, he turned totally, deliberately and knowingly away from the Lord. At the time that was perhaps the greatest spiritual blow I had even received. To this day, well over half a century later, as I think back on Alvaro and our friendship together, that blister is still very prominent. I don't expect it will ever be healed before heaven unless somehow I should find out that Alvaro has returned into the fold of the Lord Jesus Christ.

Getting up a 2:00 a.m. to go out in the snow on a freezing Montana night to save the life of a newly born lamb was not always pleasant. But the reward of saving a newborn life which probably could not have survived alone was infinitely gratifying. Joys of that nature will sustain many a missionary.

One example is the story of the deadly spiritual warfare to salvage the soul of a man who had literally sold himself to Satan. I give more detail about that in a later chapter. The spiritual warfare that night was for me far more intense than seeking to save the life of a newly born lamb out in the snowy plains of Montana. It was a very genuine battle for the soul. As I reflect on that incident, my experiences of reaching out for a newly born lamb come to mind as I recall seeing this Satan worshiper being born again into the fold of the Shepherd who loved him.

Thus the lessons I learned from hard work during my growing-up years had long-term effects in my mission work.

CHAPTER EIGHT
The Place of Good Books

Books have played a foundational role in the life of the Howard family. My father always carried a book with him to read on a train, a bus, a plane or wherever he might have a few moments of spare time. In this way he set an example that I have tried to follow throughout my life.

Reading aloud to the family was an integral part of our home life. On Sunday afternoon our father would read missionary stories and biographies to us children. We always loved the stories of John G. Paton, missionary to the cannibals of the South Sea Islands, and would frequently ask our father to read them again.

From our earliest childhood Mother would read to us. Of course she read to us the well-known nursery rhymes and children's books such as *The Wizard of Oz*, as well as the Christopher Robin and Winnie the Pooh books by A.A. Milne. She even had a songbook of A. A. Milne poems and would play them on the piano and sing them to us. For herself, she loved Charles Dickens and had a full set of his books. I believe she probably read everything that he ever wrote.

Partly because of this great heritage, three of us children became writers. Elisabeth Elliot is well known as a best-selling author whose works have been read widely for nearly 50 years. Our brother Tom has written books and articles that have appeared in various publications and scholarly journals. I have written ten books, although I often say that being the brother of a best-selling author has not made me a best-selling author.

We are the fourth generation of authors, since our father, grandfather and great grandfather all wrote books. My son, David Jr., has written four or five scholarly books as an Old Testament professor at Bethel University. Thus he is the fifth generation of our family's writers.

When our father was the editor of the *Sunday School Times*, which existed from 1859 to 1967, it entered into the theological controversies of the early to mid-twentieth century and was acknowledged by many at that time as the voice of evangelicalism. As a writer he was scrupulously careful in the use of language, grammar, vocabulary and spelling. He would not permit his children to misuse these and insisted on correcting us when we did.

He kept a one-volume dictionary/encyclopedia within arm's reach of the dinner table. We often had lively and interesting family discussions around the table on a wide variety of topics such as theology, current events, literature, music, life styles, biblical stories, history and more. Whenever there was a disagreement on the use of vocabulary, spelling or some fact that should be verified, he would reach for the dictionary/encyclopedia and say, "Well, let's settle this right now and get it right."

His way of teaching had a profound impact on us children. Consequently, reading has had a seminal influence on my life. During our first year on the mission field I began keeping a record of every book I read. I averaged about 40 to 50 books a year. Many have had a significant life-changing influence on me.

(For a listing of some of the books that have especially influenced me, see the index in the back of this book.)

CHAPTER NINE
Toronto 1946

It was the week of December 27 to January 2, 1945–46, and the temperature was near zero degrees Fahrenheit. In Toronto, Canada, the streets and sidewalks were icy, the wind chill severe. However, 575 college and university students from across the United States and Canada were at the University of Toronto, part of a history-making event, although we were scarcely aware of the significance of that event as yet. I was one of those students.

We were attending the Convention for Missionary Advance, which was the forerunner of what would become the Urbana Convention sponsored by InterVarsity Christian Fellowship (IVCF).

In 1945, IVCF had merged with the Student Foreign Missions Fellowship (SFMF), which was an organization founded in 1936 by students and subsequently directed and administered by students. The purpose of SFMF was to challenge and recruit students for overseas mission outreach. IVCF, which had come to the United States from Canada in 1939-40, had missions as one of its major purposes.

Soon IVCF/SFMF began to consider holding a nationwide convention to challenge students, particularly of the post-World War II generation, for world outreach in missions. Similar conventions had been held previously by the older Student Volunteer Movement from 1886 on. Plans were made to hold a convention to challenge students about their worldwide responsibility.

While a sophomore at Wheaton College, I attended the Toronto Convention. It was an exhilarating opportunity to mingle with hundreds of like-minded men and women interested in missions. The program reminded us of our "responsibility to take the gospel to every creature." Through well-known speakers who were making a difference in missions around the world, and through interaction with other students, God touched my heart and I felt led to respond to the call for unqualified missionary service. I signed a card pledging to plan and prepare for missions. The date was 1946, and from then on that card was a constant reminder of one of the most significant decisions I ever made. It shaped the rest of my life.

I attended the next convention in 1948, which had moved to Urbana, Illinois, while a senior at Wheaton College. Following my graduation, C. Stacey Woods, General Secretary of InterVarsity, recruited me to become "Missions Staff Member" of IVCF, a position I held for three years before going to Latin America as a missionary. During one of those years I served as assistant director of the third convention, "Urbana 1951." And later, after 15 years as a missionary in Latin America, I would return to direct the Urbana conventions during the decade of the 1970s.

That post-World War II generation of students, many of whom were veterans of the war, ushered in an amazing outreach of missions in the latter half of the 20th century. This was the greatest forward movement of missions in the entire modern era.

CHAPTER TEN
A Man and His Influence

His head began to nod slowly as one of his students droned on in translating a passage from the Greek New Testament. It would appear that Dr. Merrill C. Tenney was falling asleep, quite oblivious to how the student was translating the passage. But then the student made a mistake and suddenly Dr. Tenney snapped to attention. He said, "Hold it. You've missed that one. Let's correct it." The professor had been quite alert; his mind was so quick that nothing was missed.

Merrill C. Tenney was Dean of the Graduate School at Wheaton College and Chair of the Department of Bible and Theology in the undergraduate school. His mind was like a steel trap. He could catch even the tiniest nuance in Greek translation, theological discussion or exegetical development. To study under Dr. Tenney required constant vigilance and hard work. Any student who was not willing to dig deeply into the material would not make it in his classes.

As an undergraduate, I took every course under Dr. Tenney that I could fit into my schedule. When I pursued the M.A. degree in Theology, it was my good fortune to have him as my thesis advisor. I had to work hard to meet his standards. One of my classmates was Dale Oxley, a former U.S. Marine who had fought in the islands of the Pacific during the war. In later years, Dale and I would often compare notes about Dr. Tenney's courses and how much they helped us during our years of missionary service. Dr. Tenney did not just fill us with information, which he easily could have done. Rather, he taught us the skills of biblical exegesis and how to use the available tools for such study.

One day, years later, I received through my mission society a generous financial gift from Dr. Tenney. Later I found that he had gone to his heavenly reward and realized that he had been preparing for this departure by parceling out his assets to others. The fact that he chose one of his former students to benefit from his giving shows his personal interest in his disciples. He was not an "ivory tower" scholar. He knew us and loved us.

One time in Colombia we were facing one of the most divisive and difficult problems we'd ever encountered. It was then that I was able to call upon what I had received from Dr. Tenney, even to consult with him personally in a way that was very helpful.

My son, David Jr., is today a professor of Old Testament and Hebrew in a theological seminary. He has heard me tell how much Dr. Tenney and other professors meant to me in my graduate years and how I was often able to apply on the mission field what I had learned from him and others. I have heard David say that he feels that God's calling to him today is similar. God has led him into the scholarly world of teaching other men and women who are preparing to serve the Lord around the world. He desires that just as Dr. Tenney influenced my life in world missions, he may also be able to influence the lives of many future missionaries.

CHAPTER ELEVEN
The Discipline of Sports

"This match has ended in a tie. We will now wrestle two overtime periods of two minutes each." This announcement came over the loudspeaker at a wrestling match. I could scarcely believe my ears. This was my first collegiate wrestling match. I had made the varsity team in my freshman year at Wheaton College, and our first intercollegiate meet was held at the University of Illinois in Urbana.

In those days a match was nine minutes long in three periods of three minutes each. That proved to be so strenuous on the wrestlers that the rules were later changed, and today a match is only seven minutes long. Overtimes are wrestled only in tournaments, not in dual meets. Today a tie is left as a tie, but that was not true in those days. So in my first match I had already wrestled nine minutes and now I was faced with four minutes more. We had one minute to rest before the start of the overtime period.

I flopped down on the edge of the mat feeling utterly exhausted and without much hope that I might actually win this match. Two of the older wrestlers, Jim Fraser, the team captain, and Ladoit Stevens, who would be captain the next year, both jumped down beside me and began to talk excitedly. They burst out, "Dave! You HAVE this guy! He is far more tired than you are. We can tell. We know from our own experience, and you are winning. Hang in there, and you will win!!"

In overtime, I somehow turned my opponent onto his back and he immediately became like a deflated balloon. With a gasp of expiring breath he lay flat, and I won by a pin.

Of course I had more matches in the next four years. I had my share of wins, but also losses. Some wins were exciting, while some losses were embarrassing and discouraging. I am grateful for two team captains who instilled in me the confidence that I could win. It gave me a great start for a college career, and it was a strong example of the need to instill encouragement and confidence in others.

The importance of encouraging others who may be discouraged or feeling defeated in missionary work is vital. Many times as a mission executive I had to lift the spirits of missionaries who were feeling on the verge of defeat. The struggles for them may have been deep and hard, and the temptation to quit was real. I needed to encourage them and show them that they could win.

Dealing with disappointment and defeat was hard, but good for me. In later life I believe it helped me handle difficult situations, discouragement and defeats of a spiritual or emotional nature. The lessons of discipline, perseverance, hard work and positive mental attitude were especially helpful when trudging through the jungles of Colombia on muddy trails or climbing the high Andes Mountains. Having the stamina to take one more step was like hanging in there in the final minutes of an exhausting wrestling match.

No college wrestler will ever be a winner if he is in poor physical condition. The same is true for missionaries, especially those who are in rural and pioneer work. The need to keep going in the midst of exhausting physical exertion can be the difference between victory or defeat.

While on the field I found it necessary to stay in good physical condition. We lived near the beach in Cartagena, Colombia, and that was an ideal place for me to go jogging and swimming. That stood me in good stead in the midst of draining travel or work. Knowing from my wrestling days that I could always make just one more effort to keep going came in handy in such times on the field.

Since we are to be good stewards of what God gives to us, this includes the stewardship of our bodies. The missionary who neglects this area of life will pay the consequences sooner or later in unfortunate ways. Our physical condition often affects our emotional and spiritual condition as well. We are in spiritual warfare. Knowing how much such warfare can drain the soul and then the body, missionaries need to realize that our tripartite life is intricately intertwined between body, soul, and spirit.

Over the more than half a century since I wrestled my last collegiate match, I have been profoundly thankful for the physical, emotional and spiritual lessons learned on the mat. Wrestling is a strenuous and demanding sport, and the discipline to stay in top physical condition was essential. Even though I realize that "we wrestle not against flesh and blood," as Paul reminds us in Ephesians 6:12, and our true wrestling is against principalities and powers in the world, nevertheless I am grateful for lessons learned in wrestling against flesh and blood.

Another totally different sport was also valuable to me. Wrestling is an individual sport, where the athlete is totally alone. He wins or loses on his own. But I was also privileged to play four years of soccer at Wheaton College. Soccer is a team sport. One wins or loses along with ten other teammates. I am thankful that I had the opportunity to participate in a team sport, as there are many lessons to be learned in this discipline.

Soccer requires an attitude of cooperation. One player never won a soccer game on his own; it takes a full team to play to win. In my first year at Wheaton we were not very strong as a team, although improvement was seen as we moved along. In more recent years, under outstanding coaching, Wheaton has won several national championships with both men's and women's soccer teams. This has always been when good teamwork prevailed.

In my years in Christian work, both on the mission field and in the homeland, I have seen the indispensability of cooperation in the work of the Lord. It is always sad when there are those in Christian work who refuse to cooperate with others who have the same goals and desires. On the other hand, it is always exciting to see the church move forward when all the members of the body of Christ are in one accord.

Christ prayed "that all of them may be one, Father...so that the world may believe...May they be brought to complete unity to let the world know that you sent me and have loved them even as you have loved me" (John 17: 21-23 NIV).

CHAPTER TWELVE
He Never Raised His Voice

The burly ex-Marine came thundering around third base heading full speed for home plate. The catcher of the opposing team was primed to receive the throw from the outfield. Ball and ex-Marine and catcher all collided at the same instant in a wild tangle of arms and legs. In a flash, fists were flying between the two players. The ex-Marine represented Wheaton College, a Christian school where fighting with opponents was strictly forbidden.

Instantly Dr. Charles C. Brooks, the Dean of Students at Wheaton College, jumped off the bench where he had been sitting and, racing to home plate, jumped between the two fighters. The ex-Marine, who had been in combat during World War II, tried to push the dean away. He said, "Get out of here, Dr. Brooks. Go back to the bench where you belong."

In a firm voice, backed up with physical restraint, the dean told the Marine, "I am not going back to the bench. You will come back to the bench and get out of this fight." Then he dragged the hotheaded Marine back to the bench with him.

That incident gave me a new insight into the character of Dr. C. C. Brooks. He was a mild, soft-spoken man who never raised his voice. The picture most of us had of him was of a godly man of integrity who would deal sympathetically with students no matter what the issue. I had never seen him become angry or upset. But when that Wheaton student got into that fight, Dr. Brooks was right there to defend the integrity of Wheaton and restrain the student.

The usual picture of Dr. Brooks that comes to my mind is of a man whose primary purpose in life was to serve the Lord with all his heart, soul and mind and to serve the students of Wheaton College in the most loving and understanding way possible. Dr. Brooks hated disciplinary action, but he did not shy away from it when it became necessary. There were times when he would give me a call and say, "Dave, can you get a couple of friends and come to my office this afternoon?" When he said that, I knew that there was some problem with a student that would require guidance and discipline.

Since I was president of the Student Council, Dr. Brooks seemed willing to confide in me and ask advice from some of us in whom he had confidence. So I would gather a few students who I knew would be willing to interact with the dean to help him decide the best way to handle a problem. Back then there was a pledge that students signed, and if a student broke that pledge, he would be disciplined, or even expelled. Dr. Brooks preferred to probe into the student's heart and mind and find out what made him break the promise he had made. He saw a student's inappropriate behavior as a deeper spiritual problem and tried to work with him to bring him into a stronger relationship with the Lord.

Dr. Brooks saw each student as an individual whom God loved and whom he also loved and wanted to help in personal growth. I have sat in his office and seen him shed tears as he struggled with how to help a student who was heading down a slippery slope and who needed a strong hand to rescue him. His desire to do everything in his power to help that student was why he would call some of us other students to give him advice on how to deal with the situation.

The lessons I learned from seeing Dr. Brooks always looking at the individual and not just at the rules have stood me in good stead throughout my life. I have tried to emulate him in seeing my colleagues and others with whom I have ministered as people who need understanding, love and compassion in order to grow in the Lord. His example has always been before me in my ministry.

One time we had contact with a situation where a Christian worker was found to be guilty of serious sin. That person's overseer tried in a loving and understanding way to bring about repentance and correction. The overseer saw the heart need of the one who had failed.

However, a young missionary became very upset that the overseer did not take stronger direct action and fire the one who had fallen into error. This newer missionary did not understand the cultural implications or the heartfelt efforts being made by the overseer. The result was a complete breakdown of communication and fellowship between the younger missionary and the overseer.

The younger missionary could have learned some good lessons from a man like Dr. Brooks, who always tried to find the cause of a problem rather than stick to the rules in a rigid way. Missionaries and Christian workers can learn from the example of a godly man such as Dr. Brooks.

CHAPTER THIRTEEN
The German Submariner

He arrived as a former German prisoner of war during my junior year at college. Many of our classmates who had been in the war had seen prisoners of war, but to some of the younger men this was a new experience.

This former member of the Wehrmacht was sweeping the halls and cleaning the restrooms of Blanchard Hall. Since he spoke almost no English, we could not communicate with him. He had a pleasant smile and we enjoyed greeting him in the hallways. As far as we knew, he was not a Christian, so Jim Elliott got the vision that we should start praying for him. We would get together to pray for this man of whom we knew very little. After a time he left Wheaton and we lost contact with him. We only hoped that the Lord would be working in his heart to bring him to salvation.

In 1978, I was invited by the Lausanne Committee for World Evangelization to help organize and direct a consultation on world evangelization which was to be held in Pattaya, Thailand, in 1980. Our first planning meeting was held in Bermuda. One afternoon we had some free time, so a number of us were strolling around the streets of downtown Hamilton. I was standing at the waterfront with one of the men as we looked at some of the ships tied up in port. One was a British submarine. My companion, who was from Germany, commented, "I served in Hitler's submarine corps."

I was fascinated and asked for more details. He said, "Towards the end of the war, as the Allies were sweeping across Europe and crossing the Rhine River into Germany, Hitler pulled most of us off the submarines and naval vessels to put us in the front lines as infantry. I was in Holland when I was wounded. That was the best thing that could have happened to me, as I was abandoned by our troops in retreat and was captured by the British. They sent me to a hospital in

England. The rest of my contingent were sent eastward and were captured by the Russians. Most of them were never heard of again."

I asked him what happened next. He explained that he had gone from England to the United States for a period of time. His name was Peter Schneider and he was then the director of the Billy Graham Evangelistic Association offices in Germany and the editor of *Entschidung*, the German edition of *Decision Magazine*. He spoke perfect English and served as Billy Graham's interpreter whenever Billy preached in Germany.

Suddenly my mind began to spin backwards, dredging up memories from thirty years before. Wasn't Peter Schneider the name of the man we had prayed for when we were students? I asked, "Peter, were you ever at Wheaton College in Illinois?" "Why yes," he replied, "I worked there as a janitor sweeping floors and cleaning restrooms." My heart leaped with joy. "Peter," I asked, "Were you a Christian at that time?" "No," he replied, "I became a Christian later at a YMCA camp in Wisconsin. When I was at Wheaton I knew almost nothing of the gospel."

I said, "Peter, you would have no way of knowing this, but I must tell you what happened during your time there. Jim Elliott (whose name Peter knew as one of the five martyrs in the Ecuador jungles in 1956) got a vision to pray for your salvation. He organized several of the students, including me, to pray that you would come to know the Lord. We could not witness to you because we didn't know German. But we prayed for you during those days."

My excitement knew no bounds. Here I was standing at the waterfront in Bermuda with a key evangelical leader from Germany for whom we had prayed years before at Wheaton. I could only bow in humble thankfulness for the way God had so abundantly answered those prayers. We never could have dreamed where this janitor, former prisoner of war, would end up. And Peter was equally moved and grateful as he realized how a few young men, whom he never really knew, had played a role in bringing him to salvation and the profound ministry that he had.

Scripture tells us, "'For my thoughts are not your thoughts, neither are your ways my ways,' declares the LORD. 'As the heavens are higher than the earth, so are my ways higher than your ways and my thoughts than your thoughts'" (Isaiah 55:8–9 NIV).

Over the years I have learned slowly but steadily that God does not always answer prayer quickly. His timing may be far different than mine. This story of Peter Schneider is one of the most gratifying examples of God answering prayer that I have seen in my life.

There are, however, other instances where I had prayed earnestly for a friend but never saw the answer to that prayer. In the case of Peter Schneider, I cannot honestly say that I had prayed steadily for him for thirty years. But our prayers for him at Wheaton College thirty years earlier were fervent. There are others for whom I prayed consistently for a period of time and then dropped those prayers. I find it comforting to know that God has heard my prayers even though I have not seen the answer. Someday in heaven I will know the results.

Patience on my part plus a restful peace in knowing that my loving Father is sovereign and will do His work in His own time are comforting to me, especially when His answer seems long delayed or perhaps denied.

CHAPTER FOURTEEN
"It's O.K., Sonny Boy"

It was the last week of school. Final exams and "comps" for seniors were over. A group of us seniors decided it was time to have a last fling and have some fun. As ideas of what to do began to jell, we picked up on a local event and built from there.

That week there had been a jailbreak from the DuPage County jail in downtown Wheaton. This could be the excuse for some fun. So we all got dates for a particular evening, some with steady girlfriends, others with first-time dates. As we gathered on campus we talked as though we had no firm plans but were deciding right then. We tossed around some suggestions about what to do and then someone said, "I've got an idea. You know those escaped criminals from the jail. I'll bet they're hiding in the cemetery. Let's go down and hunt for them."

Much to the consternation of our dates who protested vigorously, all the fellows agreed that this was a great idea. So we piled into a couple of cars and headed for the cemetery. It was an exceptionally dark night with no moon, which made the setting even better. We parked at the entrance and started in, slowly moving deeper into the foreboding surroundings of the cemetery. The reluctance of the young women we were with was growing by the minute.

Suddenly we saw two figures jump up from behind some bushes and start to fight with each other. What our dates didn't know was that the two guys arguing and then fighting were Ed McCully and Jack Swanson. Suddenly one yelled, "I'm going to give it to you right now," and the reply, "No, No! Please, don't." At that point a pistol shot rang out and one of the men (Jack Swanson) slumped to the ground. Ed McCully, himself a track star, had brought one of the starter pistols used at a track meet.

We yelled, "Let's get him," and took off after Ed who was running off, leaving the women behind in that eerie, dark cemetery frozen on the spot. After a few minutes we returned and said one of them had gotten away but the other was lying either dead or wounded on the ground. One of the women was Muriel Thompson, a graduate nurse. So we said, "Muriel, you're a nurse; you have to help this man."

She protested, "There's no way I'm going over there." We told her, "Muriel, you have no choice; you have to take care of a needy human being." So she followed us to where Jack Swanson was lying face down on the ground with his arms covering his head. Muriel knelt down and felt around his body to see if there was any blood. Jack was shaking as he tried to stifle his laughter. Then she began to stroke Jack's head, speaking softly to assure him that everything would be all right, that we would take care of him. She kept calling him, "Sonny Boy."

The rest of us were beside ourselves with trying to hold back our laughter, and we knew Jack could not hold it in much longer. So we agreed to get him to the car so that we could take him to the hospital. So keeping Jack's head covered, we carried him to one of the cars and put him in the back seat. We told Muriel that she had to get into the back seat to look after him while we drove to the hospital. She protested about getting in the car with a man who might be one of the escaped criminals. We forced the issue and reluctantly she got into the back seat with him.

At that point Bob Mitchell turned on the car's dome light. Jack, whose face was a few inches from Muriel's, looked right at her and said, "Helloooo, Muriel." I have seldom seen anyone as angry as Muriel was when she jumped out of the car screaming at us, "Oh, you awful guys. I can't believe you would do this." She stomped around for several minutes venting her anger while we guys were rolling around on the grass overcome with laughter. To this day we still greet Muriel with "Sonny Boy" whenever we see her.

Even though we may have been known as campus rowdies, it is interesting to see what those students have done in life. Jim Elliot and Ed McCully were two of the missionaries martyred by the Waodani (Auca) Indians in the jungles of Ecuador in 1956. Jack Swanson earned his PhD and became superintendent of schools in Oak Park, Illinois. Bob Mitchell became president of Young Life in Colorado Springs. Bob Blaschke went to Benin, Africa, where he translated the New Testament into a remote and difficult language. Muriel Thompson married Art Johnston and together they went to France with TEAM and later founded Tyndale Theological Seminary in The Netherlands. And I have spent 50 years in missions.

The humor and fun-loving nature of so many of those involved in this particular story stood them in good stead years later on the mission field. There is a beautiful DVD entitled *Beyond the Gates of Splendor* that tells the story of the five men who were murdered by the Waodani Indians in Ecuador in 1956. As mentioned above, two of those men, Jim Elliot and Ed McCully, were involved in the cemetery prank. Ed was our senior class president and Jim was president of the Student Foreign Missions Fellowship. In the DVD, the five widows discuss at some length their husbands and what actually took place in that story.

At one point, Olive, the widow of Pete Fleming, tells with great laughter herself how Jim Elliot and Ed McCully, when they got together, were irrepressible clowns. Several stories are told on that DVD about the humor of these men. It is interesting to see how, as they were preparing to attempt to reach this remote, savage tribe, whom they knew might kill them, their sense of humor kept coming to the fore. Their humor was never used to belittle the seriousness of their missionary task; however, it was greatly used to alleviate the constant tensions under which many missionaries have to work.

It was my privilege also to serve as an assistant general director under the leadership of Dr. Horace (Dit) Fenton, who was general director of the Latin America Mission. Dit Fenton had as great a sense of humor as anyone I have ever known. Often in difficult administrative sessions, when we would be discussing some deep issues that pressed heavily upon us, Dit's gift of humor would be used spontaneously to break up a heavy session. We were often convulsed in gales of laughter in a way that would wonderfully relieve the tension and get us back on track to carry on with the seriousness of our mission. Missionaries who have no sense of humor will be in for a difficult life.

The Bible says, "A cheerful heart is good medicine" (Proverbs 17:22 NIV). "A feast is made for laughter" (Ecclesiastes 10:19 NIV). I've learned that a good practical joke can be good medicine or even a feast.

CHAPTER FIFTEEN
The Love of My Life

"When you come to Wheaton College next year, I have the nicest little girl picked out for you." My sister Elisabeth wrote this to me during my senior year of high school. Elisabeth was one year ahead of me and was in her freshman year at Wheaton. A freshman girl who lived next door to Elisabeth had impressed my sister with her sparkling personality, physical beauty and commitment to the Lord.

Fortunately, Elisabeth never told me her name. Had she told me, she would have been the last person I would have wanted to date. There was no way I was going to have my sister pick out girls for me.

I vividly recall my first Sunday at Wheaton. After church I met my sister and a couple of other friends to have lunch together at the college cafeteria. After lunch we strolled across to North Hall, the women's dorm where Elisabeth lived, to sit in the lounge for a while and chat. In those days there was only one phone for the entire dorm and it was located in a small office just off the lounge. The students who lived in the dorm had to take turns sitting there to take incoming phone calls. They called it "desk duty."

As I walked past that little office, I saw what to my mind was just about the most beautiful girl I had ever seen. She was sitting quietly at the desk by the phone and glanced up at us as we passed. She and Elisabeth greeted each other. I was overwhelmed with how she looked, sparkling eyes, fresh and smooth complexion and warm captivating smile. I made a point of getting her name, Phyllis Gibson.

In those days I had a job in the college cafeteria serving desserts in the food line. I began noticing that Phyllis would come through at a certain time for lunch several days a week. I would anticipate the time and keep watching for her. At first we would nod politely at each other. Then we began to smile and greet one another. Aside from these casual greetings, we had no other contact. So I had to content myself with greeting her several days a week in the food line.

One day we did run into each other in a hallway and stopped to talk. With a rather hesitant approach she said, "Dave, you wouldn't want to go to the North Hall dorm party with me, would you?" Each fall and spring the dormitories would have parties and this gave the girls two times in the year when it was expected that they would invite the boys. She told me afterwards how difficult this was for her. She absolutely hated inviting a fellow for a date.

Later I discovered that Elisabeth had put her up to inviting me. Anther girl in that dorm was announcing to all around that she was going to invite Dave Howard to the dorm party. Elisabeth knew that particular girl would not appeal to me and also had it in her mind that Phyllis was the girl for me. So she set this up.

The dorm party was to be a picnic in Glen Ellyn, the town next to Wheaton. We were to hike from Wheaton to a park for the picnic. The day before the party, however, I suffered a severe "charley horse" in my right thigh from a hard kick while playing soccer. It was so painful that I knew I could not walk that distance. So I called Phyllis and told her. Before I could explain, she interrupted with, "Oh, that's fine. Don't worry. We'll just forget it." It almost sounded as though she was relieved not to have a date with me.

However, it was not my purpose to break the date but to find out if someone would be driving and would give us a ride. As it turned out, the Dean of Women was driving in her car and carrying most of the picnic supplies. She agreed to take us.

Phyllis and I were crammed into the back seat of the Dean's car along with the hot dogs, buns, potato chips, drinks and other supplies. We were jammed so close that our faces were only inches apart. I really enjoyed the "discomfort" of being squeezed so tightly into that back seat with Phyllis.

During the next three years we had many more dates. However, it was difficult to get a date with Phyllis because she was one of the most popular girls on campus. Not only was she beautiful but also she had a sparkling personality and the guys knew that a date with Phyllis would be an enjoyable time.

In those days the biggest social event of the year was the Washington banquet held on George Washington's birthday. For two years I tried to get a date with Phyllis for that banquet, but each time I was too late. She had already been invited by somebody else.

In her senior year I decided that I would not risk being told again that I was too late. So in October, I invited her for the banquet in February and she accepted. It was four months ahead of the event but I was determined not to miss this last chance. I still have a photo taken of us at the table during that banquet. During my senior year I had that photo on my dresser in the dorm. My close friend and buddy, Jim Elliott, saw that picture. He said to me, "Do you like having that picture there?" "Of course," I replied, "Why not?" He said it was so distracting that he couldn't imagine getting anything else done with a picture like that on my dresser. Four years later, when Phyllis and I got engaged, Elisabeth told me that Phyllis was the one she had picked out for me before I came to Wheaton.

CHAPTER SIXTEEN
That Special Time of Love

———

When Phyllis graduated from Wheaton College in 1948, I still had one more year to go. I don't think I dated anybody else except Phyllis during her senior year, but she was being courted by other men. After she graduated, Phyllis entered Prairie Bible Institute for one year of intensive Bible study. Phyllis and I did not correspond, so I figured that my friendship with her, while enjoyable during our college years, was now over.

Toward the end of my senior year, I began to have a strange feeling. Throughout the entire year, whenever I had a date with another girl I realized that I was constantly comparing her with Phyllis. I could not understand why this was happening. Why had I not been able to forget Phyllis?

One day during the summer of 1949, after my graduation, my father and I were driving together in New Hampshire. Suddenly a car passed us going in the other direction and I caught a quick glimpse of the driver and his companion who sat with her head on his shoulder. In that split second the girl looked to me exactly like Phyllis. Could it have been Phyllis, who lived in Montana? That brief incident threw me into an emotional tailspin. If that actually was Phyllis with that guy in the car, why did it bother me so much? Why should I care?

So I began to wonder if perhaps I might really be in love with Phyllis. How could this be? I started to pray about this. After some weeks, when I was unable to get Phyllis out of my mind, I decided to put out a fleece. I asked God for something totally unexpected to happen. I asked God that if he wanted me to marry Phyllis, to have my mother speak to me about her. This was really something way out there because my mother didn't even know Phyllis. They had met just once at the graduation of my sister Elisabeth.

The next day we were having our daily family devotions. We sang a hymn, my father read from the Bible, we all knelt down as he prayed, and we ended by saying the Lord's Prayer together. My mother jumped up from her knees, turned to me and blurted out, "Dave, what's the matter with Phyllis Gibson?" I was utterly astounded and asked, "What do you mean?" My mother replied, "Why don't you marry her?" I started to mumble something innocuous and she said, "Well, let's sit down and talk about this."

Mother asked me a lot of questions about Phyllis, my thoughts about her, how I felt. After about an hour my mother sat back laughing and said, "Dave, it's obvious to me that you are in love with Phyllis but just don't know it. Why not go ahead and ask her to marry you?" A day or two later during my own devotional time when I was reading *The Daily Light*, I read this verse: "When I passed by thee and looked upon thee, behold thy time was the time of love" (Ezekiel 16:8 KJV). It was as though the Lord spoke almost audibly to confirm for me that, yes, it was time for love to blossom in my life.

I began to wonder how I could go to see Phyllis, who lived in Montana while I was living in New Jersey. But in God's gracious timing I was just joining the staff of InterVarsity Christian Fellowship as Missions staff member. That meant that I would be traveling all over the United States and Canada challenging students about commitment to missions. My first assignment was in Colorado. While in Colorado, there was about a week of free time at the opening of the school year and I asked for permission to go to Montana during that week. I sent Phyllis a telegram and took the train to where she was living with her father and stepmother near Fromberg, Montana.

Phyllis grew up in Montana on a ranch. Both sides of her grandparents had been homesteaders in the rocky soil of south-central Montana. Their ranches were hacked out of the hard soil in that area, and Phyllis grew up knowing what truly hard work was. She spent a lot of her time as a growing-up girl hoeing beans on the ranch. Living in Montana, she had contact, as her parents and grandparents did, with the Crow Indians. She spent time climbing in the rocky hills around the area hunting for Indian arrowheads, which she could find.

When I arrived at her home, Phyllis's stepmother prepared a marvelous ranchers' dinner for me, but I was so nervous that my stomach was tied in knots and I could scarcely eat anything. After dinner, Phyllis and I went for a walk in the foothills and I told her why I had come to visit. First I told her that I loved her, then I asked her if she would marry me. Phyllis was totally unprepared for a marriage proposal. She had thought that I had just come to visit an old college friend. She could not answer for several minutes. When she finally recovered from her shock, she told me that she was not ready for such a commitment. I told her that I would wait for her to answer.

For the next four days I stayed, visiting in their home while Phyllis prayed and sought counsel from others trying to determine if this was from God. Finally, before I had to return to Colorado, God gave her peace of mind and she told me that she would marry me. We went on to enjoy 53 years of married life together, raising four children.

As I look back over those years I am profoundly grateful that God gave me the right wife. I cannot imagine how I would have survived my missionary experience with its joys but also its sorrows, with its blessings but also its struggles, with its victories but also with its defeats, if I had not had the right wife. God knew who and what I needed, and I am eternally grateful for Phyllis. My strong word to every missionary candidate is that if God's plan includes a spouse for you (wife or husband), make sure you pray for God to help you to find the right one!!

CHAPTER SEVENTEEN
Phyllis: Her Ministry to Children

One of the things I noticed early on in my relationship with Phyllis, even in our college days, was her deep love for small children. Throughout her life this was very evident.

It first came to my attention when I had a date with her one day in Wheaton, taking her to an ice-cream shop in downtown Wheaton. As I was stepping up to the counter to order milkshakes for us, she was standing off to the side. A lady standing next to me at the counter suddenly poked me and pointed over to Phyllis and said, "Look at that gorgeous girl over there! Have you ever seen a more beautiful girl than that? And look at how she's talking to that little child. How sweet and kind and loving she looks."

I looked over. Phyllis was kneeling down next to a small child—perhaps one or two years old at the most—in a baby carriage, talking to this child and smiling in the sweetest possible way. She looked absolutely beautiful, and her spontaneous love for that little child was so clear.

Years later, in our work on the mission field, this love for children again came out so strongly in many different ways. She taught Sunday school the entire time we lived in Cartagena, Colombia, always teaching small children. She also taught in a school that the mission had founded in Cartagena and enjoyed so much being with the smallest children in the school.

Another area where her love for children came into play took place when we returned to Cartagena after one of our furloughs in the U.S. We discovered that a whole new housing settlement called Blaz de Lezo was growing up outside the city of Cartagena where we lived.

Phyllis began to ask immediately, "Is there any church out in the new neighborhood?" As we investigated, we discovered there was no church or evangelical witness in that neighborhood. We found out that there were about

16,000 people there and it was growing rapidly. Therefore Phyllis decided to take a couple of Sunday school teachers with her out to that area and try to round up some children off the street and see if they could get a little Sunday school going.

She took two or three from the church that we were attending at that time in the city, asking if they would go with her on Sunday afternoons to try to see what could be done in establishing an evangelical witness. They found one Christian lady who was willing to open her home. Therefore Phyllis and her companions would go on Sunday afternoons to round up children from the streets, asking them to come in, and they would teach them Bible stories in a little Sunday school.

This worked so well that it eventually developed to the place where the time with the children was moved to Sunday morning. She would go out with two or three others from the church and regularly have Bible classes for the children.

Eventually they were able to build their own little chapel in the backyard of this woman's house and even got a man from our church in the city to come out, serving as the pastor. I was involved in another type of ministry at the time and therefore I was not accompanying Phyllis in this outreach.

That little Sunday school soon developed into a formal church with its own pastor, which then developed into a mission outreach church establishing other churches in the area. Some years later, long after we had left Colombia, I was back visiting. I preached in that church where there were now eight or nine hundred people. The pastor told me that they had been instrumental in planting 30 other churches of outreach on the outskirts of the large city of Cartagena. Thus Phyllis had been used of God in the planting of a church which became a missionary outreach church even though she would claim that she herself had never planted a church.

Phyllis always wanted to have as many children as possible. When our first child was born, the doctors indicated that a caesarean operation would be necessary because of the bone structure of Phyllis, who was quite small. Consequently, because of having had one caesarean operation, all the others had to be by the same procedure. After we had had four such operations with four wonderful children, the doctors made it clear to me that it would not be wise to continue having children. They strongly urged that we have no more children. This was a very difficult time for Phyllis. She really did want more children, but I disagreed with her on this because I felt it was much more important to have four children and a wife than to have five children and no wife. She reluctantly agreed with me and so we called off any further children even though in her own heart that's what she really wanted.

Phyllis's personal spiritual life was always a challenge to me. It was interesting to see her faithfully having her own quiet time or daily devotions. In fact, there were many times when after going to bed she suddenly remembered that she hadn't spent very much time in prayer that day. Therefore she would jump out of bed, go to her knees and spend further time in prayer before sleeping. She also had a deep concern for evangelism of neighbors, children and others elsewhere.

I was aware that Phyllis kept a journal, however she did not keep it in a very organized way. After her death I took all of her journals and read through them. I was deeply moved to see what she would be writing about. We had never read each other's journals during our married life together as we felt these were private matters that should be left to the individual. As I read some of the entries in her journals, my heart was deeply saddened because I realized that at the time she was writing I was unaware of what she was thinking and what she may have been going through at that time.

Occasionally I found entries which were short and cryptic and which made me wonder all the more what she was actually talking about. What was going on in her mind at that time? It is to this day a source of sadness to me that I did not enter in more fully with her in things that she was thinking and praying about.

But my children and I were humbled and pleased when in 2003, after Phyllis died, a building was named for her at the school in Colombia where we had served for so many years. Today Colegio Latinoamericano serves 800-900 children.

The four children that God gave us have brought great joy to Phyllis and me over the years.

David Jr. received his PhD from the University of Michigan and now teaches Hebrew and Old Testament studies in Bethel University in St. Paul, MN. He has written several scholarly books on Old Testament topics. He and his wife, Jan, have two daughters.

Stephen received his MA in Education and then joined the U.S. Navy as an aviator. He rose to the rank of Commander before retiring and joining American Airlines. He has flown throughout Latin America, Europe and the U.S. He and his wife, Cindy, have three sons.

Beth, a Wheaton College graduate, raised four children and lives in North Carolina with her husband, a former U.S. Marine. She volunteers with Habitat for Humanity and reaches out to various Hispanic families and others in her area.

Michael earned his degree in Computer Science from Northern Illinois University and now works for HSBC (Hong Kong Singapore Banking Corporation) as a Data Operations Manager. He and his wife, Julie, have four children.

All four were present at the dedication of the building in Colombia to honor their mother, who had prayed faithfully for them all their lives.

SECTION TWO
Observations of A Missionary

CHAPTER EIGHTEEN
The Lord Used You in My Life

The letter came to me in March 2003 from a person whose name I had long since forgotten. But he wrote to me, saying, "I want to thank you from the bottom of my heart for the way the Lord used you in my life. That was in the early '50s while you were with IVCF. You visited our school and what a blessing you were." Then he gave me more information about himself and his family that helped me to remember.

In 1950 I was traveling around the U.S. and Canada, a Missions staff member of InterVarsity Christian Fellowship (IVCF). In the course of visiting many campuses, I spent time in the state of Washington. The letter writer, Ron Lotz, his brother Dave, his cousin Dean and his future wife, Elaine, were all students at the time. Ron told me how he had shared with me his testimony and that he wanted to be a missionary some day.

Ron wrote, "I had all missionaries in my mind on a high spiritual pedestal, and I didn't know how I could be so spiritual." He added, "You were used of the Lord to get us moving in the right direction." Then he told me the advice I had given to him. "You told me that I was like a ship tied up at a dock. The Lord could turn the helm any which way but I was still tied down. You said that I needed to cut the ropes and to get going, and then the Lord could steer my ship and get me where He wanted me. All of us followed your advice."

They all went to New York Biblical Seminary and eventually all ended up with New Tribes Mission. Dean and his wife went to Papua, New Guinea. Dave and his wife went to Bolivia. Ron and Elaine went to Brazil where he founded a school for missionary kids on the banks of the Amazon. They also founded a leper colony and started a church there. They spent 37 years there as missionaries.

Meditating on that letter and thinking about that brief visit 53 years earlier, I realized how God worked in ways that I had never known nor could have guessed.

Many years after receiving the above letter, I received a letter from a missionary in South Africa whom, as far as I can remember, I never met. He wrote in August 2002 as follows: "My first exposure to you was at Urbana (either '70 or '73) when you spoke on the prophet Jeremiah. I got hold of those tapes and listened to them many times over the next years. I am now teaching at the Bible Institute here and have quoted you a number of times from things you said on the tape."

"One quote... is the story you told about your conversation with your father asking him if having his quiet time ever became easier. I have been grateful to you for many years for sharing that story, as it has kept me going with the realization and hope that we MUST keep going in spite of the difficulty. In fact, I had just shared that story with my class again last week...."

"David, I say all this to say thank you for more than just giving us permission to use your words. They have meant much to me over the years and I pray they will now inspire many Christian leaders throughout Africa."

The message on Jeremiah, that my letter writer remembered, was not given at Urbana but rather at another IVCF conference, but this does not detract from the heart of this story. The fact that some things that were said 30 or 40 years ago were still being used of God to reach far beyond the one hearer to others in Africa who would benefit by his teaching has been a source of my humble gratitude to God.

This reminds me again of how some seed planted may sprout in ways and places that we could never imagine. Sometimes God may give the encouragement of letting us hear about this later on. Or He may never let us know how the seed planted has blossomed. Our task is to trust the Lord for whatever He may choose to use, and we can wait patiently until He lets us know, either in this life or later in heaven. It is exciting to think of what we may learn in heaven about what God did here on earth far beyond our human knowledge.

CHAPTER NINETEEN
All Your Needs

When I graduated from Wheaton College in 1949, I spent a full year traveling with IVCF to campuses promoting interest in missions. During the course of that year I visited approximately 120 campuses. In those days the financial policy of InterVarsity was that all staff received salary from a central fund. If there were not enough funds to cover full salary for all at the end of the month, we all received a percentage of what our salary was to be. Several times we received only one-half of our salary. On one occasion we received one-fourth for two consecutive months.

Since I was traveling constantly and living out of a suitcase, I had no home base. I had to provide housing and meal costs out of my salary. There were times when I would wander the streets of some city carrying my suitcase, looking for a hotel room for $2.00 instead of $2.50, which was too much for me to pay.

One time I had spoken at a Bible institute in a small western Canadian town during the day and then had taken a hotel room for $1.75 that night. That left me with just enough cash for bus fare to my next assignment. The next morning I did not have enough money for breakfast. I remember looking in the window of a coffee shop, looking at the delicious donuts and smelling the aroma of the coffee.

As I walked on down the main street feeling sorry for myself, I suddenly heard a car beside me, the driver tooting his horn. It was the president of the Bible college where I had spoken. He had a handful of mail that had come for me and had driven down the main street in the hopes of catching me. In the mail was my salary check. I was able to cash it and go enjoy breakfast.

The following year, Phyllis and I were married. She worked on the staff of Wheaton College while I pursued graduate studies there. Her salary was small, and I had a small assistantship in the Physical Education Department, coaching the wrestling team. Phyllis was efficient in stretching our meager income.

One night I came home to dinner where she had provided an attractive apple salad. As I began to eat the salad, I was finding only apple skins, no meat of the apple. Finally I asked, "Phyllis, where is the rest of the apple?" She replied, "Oh, I saved the meat of the apple to make apple pie for tomorrow and just made a salad from the skins." In later years we often laughed about her ingenuity in stretching our funds with tricks like that.

That year I bought my first car. It was a 1928 Model A Ford that I got for $75.00. One day, while driving to a South Chicago IVCF meeting, the car threw a piston. A friend came and towed me back home. The day before I had checked our bank balance and found that we had $75.00. When I took the car to a garage for repair, the total bill was $74.00. So we had one dollar left. I marveled at how God had supplied our needs.

When it came time to raise support to go as missionaries to Costa Rica with Latin America Mission (LAM), we prayed that we would not have to go around asking for funds as so many had to do. One day I received a letter from a man I had never met, Gordon Purdy, director of Camp of the Woods in Speculator, N.Y. He was a member of the Board of Trustees of LAM. He saw that we would be needing support.

He said that Camp of the Woods, which is a large family camp that serves several thousand people throughout the summer, was developing a plan to support missionaries. On Sunday mornings they always had a large worship service in their auditorium. Sometimes up to 1,200 people would attend those services. An offering was taken each Sunday, and the camp wanted to use those offerings exclusively to support missionaries. Mr. Purdy wanted to know if I would be interested in coming to the camp in the summer of 1952 with the purpose of getting acquainted so that they could take on half of our total missionary support. Needless to say, Phyllis and I were delighted. We had not taken any initiative in this at all.

So I spent the summer of 1952 at Camp of the Woods, making wonderful friends who are still close friends to this day. Phyllis was unable to be with me, as our first son, David Jr., was born in July. I went out to Montana to be with her at the time of his birth but returned to camp at the end of the summer for final arrangements.

While I was in Montana, I went to the church Phyllis had attended as a high school student. On my first Sunday there I met the pastor in the hallway. He greeted me with, "Dave, good to see you. What are you doing these days?" I replied that we were preparing to leave soon for the mission field. Immediately he asked, "Do you have all your support yet?" I replied, "Well, we have half of it promised by Camp of the Woods." He said, "Great, I think we will take the other half. We have been looking for more missionaries to support, and you and Phyllis will be just the right couple."

So without our raising a finger the Lord provided our full support to get to the field. I am painfully aware that God does not choose to work that way with all missionaries. Others have to struggle, agonize, pray and "beat the bushes." I fully understand this. I can only say that in our case God chose to provide through those two groups.

In 1960 we were then working in Colombia where there was a severe epidemic of hepatitis. Ten of our missionaries, including me, were suffering from the illness. In my case I had tried to keep working instead of getting bed rest, and as a result developed a severe case.

One of our mission nurses, Fran Reed, would come by every other day to give me shots of dextrose, but I was slipping into deep depression because I was not able to recover. I kept having relapses. Fran noticed this and decided to take action. She said, "O.K., Mr. Field Director, I'm giving orders around here now. I'm moving into your house. I'm taking over your car, your house and your children. You and Phyllis are getting out of here. I don't care where you go, but get out. And don't come back until you are fully recovered."

Three days before, we had received in the mail a large anonymous personal gift of money. It was specifically designated "for personal use, not to be put into the mission work." I said to Phyllis, "What are we going to do with this? We don't need this personal money." But when Fran ejected us from our house, Phyllis and I were able to take that money and go off to a remote beach near Santa Maria. We spent nearly two weeks there, sleeping long hours, eating the type of protein meals needed, lounging on the beach and soaking up the sun. That anonymous gift had provided the entire amount we needed for that time of recuperation.

Years later, during my years as International Director of the World Evangelical Fellowship (WEF), my work required me to travel extensively around the world. I averaged about 16 countries each year for a ten-year period. I was so tired of jet travel that one time in Europe I decided to take a train from Budapest to Rome so that I could read, rest and enjoy the countryside. It was an overnight trip.

The train left Budapest about 6:30 a.m. and was scheduled to arrive in Rome in the late morning of the next day. I did not bother getting breakfast as

I assumed I could eat in the dining car. On taking my compartment, I asked the porter in which direction I would find the dining car. In broken English he said, "Restaurant? No." So I knew I was going to be stuck with no food until about noontime the next day.

Late in the afternoon I was feeling quite hungry and was realizing that there was no hope of getting something to eat until the following day. As I was sitting in my compartment, I prayed out loud, "Lord, You know I am very hungry. I don't expect you to send the ravens as you did for Elijah, but it surely would be nice if You could get me something to eat."

Twenty minutes later that porter came into my compartment with a tray. On the tray were a large sausage omelet, a cup of coffee, a chunk of bread and an apple. He put it down in front of me, turned and walked out before I could thank him. I never saw him again on that trip. Where he got that food and why he brought it, I don't know, except that God supplied my need. I once told this story to my eight-year-old grandson, Frankie. He said, "Grandpa, I think that was an angel dressed up like the porter." Maybe he was right.

There are other wonderful accounts about God supplying the needs of missionaries and other Christians. From my earliest childhood I have heard many such exciting stories about God's intervention and help. I have tried over the years to apply the truth of Philippians 4:19, "And my God will meet all your needs according to his glorious riches in Christ Jesus" (NIV). I know other missionaries who have found this to be true for them as well.

I believe that this is a promise to be claimed by all of us, realizing that God promises to meet all our *needs*, not necessarily giving us all we may wish we had. Properly applying that promise to our lives will lead to endless blessing.

CHAPTER TWENTY
Eliphaz: A Confession to Make

It was the final service of the weeklong conference at Camp of the Woods in July 1970. I was the speaker for the week and had used the book of Job as the basis of the messages. Each day I had taken one of the characters in the book and developed his argument in the dialogue with Job. Thus we studied Job himself plus each of his friends, Eliphaz, Bildad, and Zophar. We also studied Elihu, winding up with the powerful discourse of God Himself at the end of the book.

On Friday morning after my final message, Gordon Purdy, director of the camp, stepped up to the podium and said with deep emotion, "I have a confession to make. I was Eliphaz."

He went on to explain that in 1952, when we were heading for Latin America, Camp of the Woods had taken on a part of our support. But when we returned home from Latin America in 1968 to work as Missions staff member of InterVarsity Christian Fellowship to direct the Urbana missions conventions, this meant that we were no longer located overseas. Even though my ministry was totally related to missions, especially through the Urbana conventions, plus my personal ministry of challenging students for missions, we were no longer overseas missionaries. Consequently Camp of the Woods decided to drop our regular financial support. Nevertheless they continued to be close friends with us and in 1970 invited me to be the speaker for a full week in July. So even though we were not receiving the missionary support which we had enjoyed for fifteen years, our personal relationships were as close and warm as ever.

Now something had struck Gordon Purdy from my message on Eliphaz. Eliphaz's principle was that God always punishes the sinner. Job is suffering, so obviously he must have sinned. Gordon explained, "When Dave and Phyllis went to Latin America, we were thrilled to take on their support. We have supported them for fifteen years. We felt that God had called them to Latin America and that is where they should stay. Like Eliphaz, I felt that God does not change. Therefore when they returned to work in the United States, I felt that they had made a mistake and were missing God's calling. Since God's calling does not change, according to my Eliphaz frame of mind, they were out of God's will. Therefore we dropped their support last year."

Then Gordon went on to say, "However, now I realize that I was making the same mistake that Eliphaz made. While God Himself does not change, at times He does change His way of working with His people. He led Dave and Phyllis to Latin America, but I see that He has now changed His direction for them. He has given Dave a broad ministry with IVCF in challenging students to get involved in the mission outreach of the church. So they are still missionaries. Therefore we are taking them on again and we will enthusiastically support them in their present ministry."

From that day until our retirement, Camp of the Woods supported us faithfully. However, God does not work the same way for every missionary. Having been in mission administration I can understand how hard it is for some to raise their support. Many denominations provide for their candidates through a common fund with monies supplied by the churches. But many societies require the individuals to provide their support through local churches, friends and other sources. It stretches the faith of these missionary candidates as they wait for the Lord to provide. It can also take a long time of agonizing prayer.

Occasionally a local church will provide full support for a missionary, although this is not very common. More common is to provide partial support for a number of missionaries. Certain questions need to be raised for missionary support. For example, how well does the local church know the individuals if they support a long list of missionaries? Is there a true understanding of what these missionaries are doing? Is there intelligent prayer on their behalf? How many of the church members know these missionaries and the work they are doing?

Some churches divide up their missionaries and assign them to specific small groups in the church family. The group adopts one or two for prayer and constant contact. This can be a great blessing to the missionaries as well as to the members of the small group. When the missionary is on home leave he can visit with this group to encourage them and be encouraged by them.

In some churches where the list of supported missionaries is long, there is not enough time given for missionaries to make their work known to the entire congregation. Another problem is that some churches provide only a token amount of support to many missionaries. One missionary says he visits more than 30 churches spread over a wide geographic area. This creates the need for travel over many months, especially hard on small children. It never allowed the family to become integrated into any one church.

Home leave or furlough should be a time of connecting with supporting churches but also a time for physical, emotional and spiritual renewal. Because many missionaries face fierce spiritual warfare in their work and it drains them, they need the time at home to recuperate. This cannot be done if one is visiting a large number of supporters. One old hackneyed joke among missionaries is, "I have to get back to the field to recuperate from furlough."

Today one trend that is developing in some places is for churches to limit their number of supported missionaries so that they can enter intelligently into the lives and needs of just a few. Thus they can provide for someone on home leave to spend much of that time with the church. The church becomes a home and they are able to spend time with the church getting involved in ministry there. The "Missionary in Residence" program allows for renewal that is not possible if the missionaries are traveling most of the time. And, upon returning to the field, they have the intelligent prayer support of that church.

There are also missionaries who are supported by a society that was founded for one purpose only, namely to support that missionary. The full support of that missionary comes from that group. They are totally accountable to that society and their time at home is spent with them.

The Lord provided for Phyllis and me in a rapid and easy way. Each missionary must study the sending group to which he or she applies and be convinced that they are in accord with the financial policies of that group. "God moves in a mysterious way, His wonders to perform," wrote William Cowper in the 18th century. And God has a variety of ways to provide the needs of those servants whom He calls into ministry.

CHAPTER TWENTY ONE
What about Honoraria?

When an invitation came to speak to a conference for youth in the Midwest, I was happy to join them. I was told, "Your honorarium for participation in this conference will be what comes in from the sale of the tapes of your messages."

After the first day I was informed that my sessions would be moved to a different room in the conference location. The reason was obvious to me. On the first day they had placed me in a large auditorium as they apparently had anticipated that attendance at my sessions would be large. But that was not the case, so I was moved to a smaller room. Attendance at my sessions remained sparse for the rest of the week.

After the conference they fulfilled their promise to me and sent me a check for $0.25. Since the leaders of the conference were men who enjoyed good humor, I tore the check in half and returned it to them with the comment: "I am deeply grateful for your kind generosity, but I cannot bring myself to accept this sacrifice on your part."

As I reflect back on that experience, it brings to mind the question of how churches and other Christian organizations handle the matter of compensation for those who speak and participate in their activities. There is a wide spectrum here. Some organizations ask the speaker ahead of time what policy he or she has for honoraria. Does the speaker require a specific amount? When this is asked ahead of time, it clears the air so that both the speaker and those inviting the speaker know what is expected.

Personally, I have never asked a specific amount in return for speaking. It is left up to the group inviting me, assuming that they will cover at least travel and lodging expenses. Most organizations honor this. But sometimes the speaker can end up in embarrassing situations.

More than once I have prepared to turn in an expense account only to be told that they expected that I would cover those expenses myself. Fortunately, this is the exception and not the rule.

My sister Elisabeth, who for years traveled extensively to speaking engagements, has a whole file of incredible stories of what she has encountered in this matter of honoraria. Once, when she was living in New Hampshire, she was invited to speak for several days at a conference in Ohio. She drove alone to Ohio, spoke for those days and then drove home to New Hampshire. Her total compensation was $15.00.

My own most embarrassing experience was during one furlough from Latin America. My wife and four children were traveling with me. I spoke for a week at a well-known conference ground. On the first night in the dining hall the hostess came to my table and asked for our meal tickets. I explained that I was the speaker for the week. She replied, "Well that's fine, but you are still expected to pay for your stay here."

I could not believe my ears. I was totally unprepared to pay for six people for a week including room and board. Their rationale for their policy was that they would take an offering for the speaker at the end of the week which, they assumed, would cover the expenses for the speaker and his family.

Most churches and organizations are not that way, but sometimes groups see things from their own perspective and assume that they are being generous. Once when I was invited overseas to speak at several conferences, the travel costs were quite high. The group was paying for the travel costs and wanted to get as much from my time as possible so they asked me to stay for nearly a month. I probably spoke thirty or more times during that month. At the end, the leader, who was a westerner, not a national of the country, said they wanted to do something special for me so that I could buy a gift for my wife. He gave me a check for $40.00. This was the total payment for that month of speaking. Perhaps in his mind that $40.00 was a generous offering, but I did not think so.

However, most groups are quite generous. Once I was invited to speak at the annual convention of an international organization in Mexico. The convention was in a five-star hotel on the beach at Cancun. They paid the travel for my wife and me and all expenses for nearly a week in this lovely location. I was one of many speakers and they asked for only one 30-minute message. I do not recall the total honorarium, but it was nearly twenty times what I received for the month of speaking at that other location.

The apostle Paul said, "Do not muzzle the ox while it is treading out the grain" and "The worker deserves his wages" (1 Timothy 5:18 NIV). Every church and organization has a right to set its own policy in the matter of covering expenses and honoraria. But it is important to be completely honest and aboveboard with speakers ahead of time. No speaker should be subjected to unnecessary embarrassment because of a lack of proper information. A speaker should be given the opportunity to accept or reject an invitation on the basis of adequate understanding.

There will be times when a speaker himself/herself chooses to forgo expenses and/or honoraria because of the financial situation of the group or for other legitimate reasons. A friend of mine says, "My time is like money. If I choose to give it away, that is my choice. But if someone takes it from me, that is theft."

CHAPTER TWENTY TWO
The Picture Bible

It was a keen disappointment to me. It was our first year in Colombia with the Latin America Mission after having served five years in Costa Rica. I was still a young, inexperienced missionary, especially for the Colombia field, which was vastly different from what we had seen and done in Costa Rica.

My good friend Ernie Fowler, who had spent twenty years in Colombia reaching out to remote Indian tribes, invited me to accompany him on a trip to scout out a tribe known as the Epera Indians. He had never been in their area but he knew it was in a remote jungle far from civilization. As far as he knew they had never heard the gospel. So for me the idea of trekking with a veteran missionary into a remote area to explore an un-reached tribe was thrilling. This sounded like "real missionary work" to me.

We made plans for our trip, preparing our backpacks with essential items and making arrangements for our travel. Ernie was staying in our home at that time, as his wife and children were in the U.S. for a furlough in which he planned to join them soon.

On the morning that we were to leave, I awoke and went as usual to my time of private devotions. For some reason I seemed to sense a strong restraint about our trip. Was God indicating that we should not make this trip? If so, surely He would give some indication through the Word or other aspects of my devotional time. But nothing came. The sense of restraint grew stronger, but there was no tangible word from the Lord.

I assumed that if the Lord were indicating this restraint to me, He would be doing the same for Ernie. So I went to his room and said, "Ernie, how do you feel about this trip," fully expecting him to say that he had questions about it. But to my surprise he responded, "I feel great. I'm looking forward to it." So I explained my feelings. Ernie said, "Well, let's pray about this and see what God may be saying."

After some time of intensive prayer, seeking God's will, Ernie got up off his knees and said with a certain finality, "We will not go." Then he said, "If God is placing a restraint on us, we should not make the trip." So we cancelled the trip and I wondered if we would ever know why God seemed to be preventing us from making the trip.

Three years passed. Then one day I was ministering in a remote village in the forest at a Bible conference with new believers. Two Indian brothers named Isaias and Manuel Domico came to talk to me. They told me that they were new believers, having recently heard and accepted the gospel. But they had no instruction in the Word of God and were eager to know more and to grow in grace. They had picked up some basic Spanish from having visited outside their tribal area, so we could communicate.

When I asked where they came from, to my amazement they told me that they were from the Epera tribe—the very one to which Ernie and I had hoped to go three years before. They wanted me to come into their tribe and help them understand more about the gospel.

I was thrilled. So as soon as I returned to our home in Cartagena, I contacted Ernie Fowler to tell him about this invitation. Immediately we made plans to go into this tribal area. Isaias and Manuel had explained to me how we could get there, since it was a long distance from any civilized area.

So Ernie and I took off on a four-day trek into the deep jungle. At one point in the dense forest we lost our trail but fortunately were able to find an isolated farmer from that area who was able to guide us onto the trail again. We spent the nights in our hammocks hung from trees in the forest.

On the fourth day we broke out into a clearing and found the little cluster of Indian homes. They were round huts built on stilts with high-peaked roofs of palm branches sitting just above the rushing San Jorge River. The Domico brothers welcomed us warmly, along with the rest of the small tribal group.

For the next week Ernie and I did our best to teach and disciple the two brothers. In the morning Ernie would take one of them while I took the other, and we would lead them through the simple stories of the Bible. In the afternoon we would switch partners and each take the other one for further teaching.

Ernie had brought along a Bible storybook entitled *La Biblia En Cuadros Para Niños*, which was written in English by Kenneth Taylor (founder of the Tyndale Publishing House) under the title *The Bible in Pictures for Little Eyes*. Each page had one Bible story told in simple terms with a picture to illustrate it. The brothers were thrilled as we led them along through the developing stories.

In the evening the brothers gathered the entire group of people who lived in that area for a time of fellowship and teaching. Ernie and I taught them a few simple choruses in Spanish. I had my cornet with me to play some hymns. The first time the sound of that cornet rang out through the forest all chaos erupted. Pigs, chickens, turkeys and dogs all scrambled frantically away letting out their cries of panic. Children ran in circles, screaming and rushing up to look down the bell of the cornet to try to see what was making the sound in there. Adults were equally astounded and probably frightened too. But they soon became accustomed to that strange music and actually seemed to enjoy it.

Manuel and Isaias would then tell their friends in their tribal tongue the stories they had been learning from us during the day. Although Ernie and I did not know any of their dialect, we could often follow what story they were telling because of their dramatic body language and gestures.

One day I had told Manuel the story of David and Goliath. He was entranced. He sat on the log listening with rapt attention, his eyes growing bigger and bigger as we came to the climax. That evening he told that story to the others. I had no problem following what he was saying. He described with his arms the little shepherd boy and the huge giant. His gestures were unmistakable. He demonstrated the giant's big spear and the shepherd boy's sling. He described what happened as the stone was flung and imbedded itself into the giant's forehead and the giant collapsed. The whole tribe cheered and clapped with enthusiasm at the climax. Each evening we had similar times of watching them respond to the stories of the work of God.

When it came time for Ernie and me to leave, they felled some balsam logs and built a small raft. Along with a dugout canoe and the raft they poled us down the San Jorge River to return to our homes. Over the next few years we had occasional contact with them and found that they were faithfully following the Lord.

After many years in Colombia, the Lord led Phyllis and me to leave for further ministry elsewhere. Seventeen years after our visit to the Epera, after Ernie had died, I was back in Colombia visiting my friend Victor Landero who was ministering in another area of the jungle with the Catio Indians, far removed from the Epera Indians.

One day, as Victor and I stood talking in front of his thatch-roofed house, I saw an Indian family—father, mother, three children—emerging up the trail through the forest. As they drew closer, I recognized Manuel Domico and his family. He had no idea that I was back in Colombia and I had no idea that he now lived in this region so far from his own tribe. We were thrilled to see each other and had a great time renewing our friendship.

Then I noticed that under his arm Manuel was carrying something wrapped carefully in plastic. When I inquired what it was, he opened it up and showed *La Biblia En Cuadros Para Niños,* which Ernie had left with him following our visit. Manuel had now been using this as his Bible for seventeen years. I discovered that he carried it with him wherever he went and used it to evangelize other Indians.

As I thought back on that morning during our first year in Colombia, when I was so disappointed that God had placed a restraint on Ernie and me from making an exploratory trip to the Epera Indians, I could now understand His sovereign hand in our lives. Had Ernie and I gone at that time, there would have been no "bridge" into the tribe. There were no Indians as yet who were believers. We would not have known where or how to start. The trip might well have been a total failure.

But in the meantime God had brought Isaias and Manuel to Himself, and they had invited us to come and teach them the Word of God. They were the "bridge" into that group of Indians to open the way into their hearts. Scripture tells us, "Trust in the Lord with all thine heart; and lean not unto thine own understanding. In all thy ways acknowledge him and he shall direct thy paths" (Proverbs 3:5–6 KJV). When we had trusted the Lord, He had directed our paths and the gospel entered a new area.

Several lessons have been important to me as I reflect on my friendship with the Domico brothers. First, waiting on God, not moving ahead when He was placing restraints, was important for the fulfillment of God's purpose in the lives of the Domico brothers and the Epera tribe.

Second, the power of the simple Word of God which can penetrate hearts and minds, as it did in the Epera tribe. It was thrilling to see these people respond openly to God.

Third, the faithfulness of a humble uneducated Indian in keeping a Bible story book carefully for seventeen years so that he could share its message with others was a gratifying challenge for me.

I am reminded of Isaiah 55:11, "...so is my word that goes out from my mouth; It will not return to me empty, but will accomplish what I desire and achieve the purpose for which I sent it" (NIV).

CHAPTER TWENTY THREE
Our lives in Santo Domingo de Heredia

Santo Domingo de Heredia was a sleepy little country village tucked into the foothills of the mountains surrounding San Jose when Phyllis and I moved there in 1953. We were halfway through our year of language study.

The reason for our move was twofold. Dit Fenton, field director of the LAM for Costa Rica, lived in Santo Domingo at that time. But he wanted to move back into San Jose to be closer to the mission offices. For our part, we wanted to get out into a village where we could put our efforts at using Spanish to more aggressive use. So he turned over to us the house he had rented and also gave us the use of his 1936 Ford for transportation.

There was only one family in Santo Domingo who were evangelicals, plus a tiny handful of single believers. There was no evangelical church in the village so the Fentons held a Bible study each Sunday afternoon in their home. Dit felt that we had made enough progress in our Spanish by that time for me to take over this small effort of outreach

The house was an old Spanish colonial style with a red tile roof and thick adobe walls. It opened directly out on a grassy street, as most streets in the village were unpaved. It also had its menagerie. We had a family of possums who lived under our roof above the ceiling. At night they would rush up and down across our ceiling with screams which either represented fun or fights for them.

We became intimately acquainted with cockroaches, tarantula spiders, large toads that would flop across our bedroom floor at night with loud plops, plenty of bats that would wake us up by swishing across our faces, as well as the occasional snake.

One day, when David Jr. was about two years old, he came into the kitchen urgently asking Phyllis to "come see the cow." Plenty of cows would wander past our house feeding on the grassy street. This was not unusual, so Phyllis tried to brush him off, as she was busy in the kitchen. But David was not to be put off and continued urging her to "come see the cow." So she finally succumbed and went with him into the front room that opened out onto the street. There stood a cow, calmly making herself at home in our living room. Phyllis grew up on a ranch in Montana, so cows did not intimidate her. She calmly ushered the cow out onto the street and returned to her work in the kitchen.

We had a large and lovely walled-in yard behind the house with a variety of citrus trees (grapefruit, oranges, lemons), as well as papaya and bananas. A wide selection of beautiful tropical flowers was spread throughout the yard. I once counted fourteen varieties without turning my head to look in another direction.

We had a Costa Rican gardener who mowed our lawn by hand with a machete and kept the trees and flowers in good shape. Although he was illiterate, he could tell time almost to the minute by looking at the sun. If our clock ever stopped, Phyllis would go to him and ask, "Nano, what time is it?" He would look at the sun and then tell her the time. When we checked it later, we found he was usually within five or ten minutes of the exact time.

Santo Domingo was fanatically anti-Protestant. Many houses had signs in the window that read in Spanish, "We are Catholics; we do not accept Protestant propaganda." Since I sometimes went door-to-door to distribute tracts or gospel portions, it was not unusual to have the door slammed in my face or have the tract torn up and thrown back at me.

One week we noticed that the whole town seemed to be coming by and peering in our windows. It was not at all unusual for children to peer in at us, but this particular week it was the adults as well. At the end of the week a friend asked me, "Have you had a lot of people peering in your windows this week?" "Yes," I replied, "what's going on?" He said, "Last Sunday the local priest preached a sermon against you saying that devils lived in that house and that no one should go near it." So, naturally, the village people wanted to know what devils looked like.

During our first few months in Santo Domingo a high-school student named Alvaro came and asked if I would help him with English so that he could pass his English exams to receive his high-school diploma. I gladly agreed and we began to meet regularly for lessons.

After a few weeks I told him that the finest English was found in the Bible. I asked if he would like to read the Bible with me. He was glad to do this. So we began to read portions of the Word of God that had simple English, such as the Gospel of John. After a few months of this study, Alvaro came to the place where he said he wished to accept Christ.

I was thrilled, as this would be the first person I would lead to the Lord as a missionary in Latin America. So I began to disciple Alvaro, meeting two or three times a week for study and prayer. He would go out with me in door-to-door witnessing. He took a Bible correspondence course from our seminary in San Jose. He went to a night school of the Bible in the Templo Biblico, a key church in San Jose. For two years Alvaro apparently grew rapidly in the Lord. I spent more time in mentoring him than I have ever spent with any one person before or after.

Then one night Alvaro slipped a note under my door that said in essence, "I no longer believe what you have been teaching me. I am going back to my former way of life." I was crushed and spent most of that night in weeping and prayer.

I went to Alvaro's house to try to talk to him. But his family always told me that he was not there. They obviously were covering up for him. It took me several weeks to finally run him down. When I asked him what had happened, he would not open up and give me any explanation.

For the next couple of years we saw each other occasionally. Then we were transferred to Colombia and Alvaro went off to Mexico to study medicine. He later returned to Santo Domingo as a doctor. Twelve or thirteen years later I was in Costa Rica on a visit and went to see him. I found him at home and we had a delightful visit, like old friends. However, there was no sign of spiritual life at all.

This experience was one of the times of deepest sadness and feelings of defeat that I ever had in years of missionary work. In spite of all my efforts to help Alvaro understand and grow in the Lord, the seed either died quickly or was choked out of his life.

But there were a few flickers of light in Santo Domingo. The family of Victor and Aida Barquero with their four children was the only family in which all were following the Lord. Phyllis and I had to move out of our adobe home and move back to San Jose for the health of one of our children who was suffering severe bronchial trouble due to the dampness of the adobe bricks. But we continued going out twice a week to Santo Domingo for prayer meetings and Bible studies.

Victor Barquero made his home available for meetings. He even built a small chapel beside his house, which became the first little evangelical church in that village. The family followed the Lord well. I had the privilege of baptizing and performing the marriage of Vilma, their oldest daughter. Over the years we kept in contact with the Barqueros. Don Victor is now with the Lord, and his wife, Dona Aida, has joined him in glory. But I thank the Lord for their faithfulness to Him.

Don Damian, an uneducated day laborer, also loved the Lord and worked tirelessly to witness to others. He was almost fanatical in his way of witnessing and often turned off others by his aggressive approach with the gospel. But he was faithful in doing what he believed the Lord wanted him to do.

The two and one-half years that Phyllis and I lived in Santo Domingo were years of learning a lot of lessons, both hard and pleasing, as we tried to enter into the culture and prepare for further outreach to the Latin American people to whom God had called us. They laid the foundation for the rest of our missionary experience.

I have often reflected back on my time with Alvaro and all the efforts at mentoring that were poured into his life for two years. What does one make of a situation like this? I am comforted with the words from Philippians 1:6: "...being confident of this, that he who began a good work in you will carry it on to completion until the day of Christ Jesus" (NIV).

Because Alvaro was the first person that I apparently led to Christ in Latin America, this hit me heavily and caused great searching of my heart. It has also helped me to deal with other situations when I felt defeated in kingdom work. A recognition that God is in control, that the work is His, that I am only one instrument in His powerful hands has comforted me.

Another verse has been of great encouragement. 1 Corinthians 4:2 says, "Now it is required that those who have been given a trust must prove faithful" (NIV). The word does not say *"fruitful,"* but rather, *"faithful."* Certainly God wants to see fruit as a result of the trust He has given us as missionaries. But more important than fruitfulness is faithfulness. Carrying out the trust may or may not result in fruit. My part is to remain faithful in the trust given to me.

CHAPTER TWENTY FOUR
Explosion of Short-term Missions

The year was 1957 and we were home on our first furlough, which is now called "home ministry assignment." I was invited to speak at Urbana '57. This was a pleasing honor for me since as a student I had attended the first two InterVarsity missions conventions held at Toronto in 1946 and Urbana, Illinois, in 1948. I had also served as assistant director of Urbana '51 while I was on staff at IVCF. So when the invitation came to participate in Urbana '57, I was delighted.

One afternoon, when seminars or workshops were being held all across the campus, I participated in a panel with several other missionaries. I don't recall the topic of the seminar, but one fact from that day stands out clearly in my mind.

During the course of the discussion, one of the missionaries brought up the idea that students could go overseas for a short visit, such as a summer or a few months, for some mission activity. During the five-day convention the students were being bombarded day and night with messages about missions. The emphasis was clearly that missions was a lifetime commitment. But suddenly here was a new thought. Maybe it was not necessary to think in terms of lifelong commitment. Instead, the responsibility of helping to carry out the Great Commission might be fulfilled in a matter of months.

Up to that time, none of us had ever heard of "short-term" in the context of missions. Previous generations had always thought of missions as a commitment for a lifetime. Now here was an idea that would allow one to satisfy his or her responsibility to the Great Commission during a short term.

What amazed me was that once this idea was put out on the table, it totally dominated the rest of the panel discussion. The students leaped on it with enthusiasm and did not want to discuss any other topic. As I tried to analyze what was in their minds, it almost seems as though their enthusiasm was for the possibility of "getting the monkey of missions off my back" in a short time.

Since this was a new concept, it became quite intriguing to see the response. At least another decade or more passed before the concept of "short-term missions" really became an accepted part of mission recruitment. I am not sure if an exact date can be given for the beginning of this movement, but I can say that as an observer and participant in missions since the late 1940s and early 1950s, Urbana '57 was the first time it ever came to my attention.

Today short-term missions occupy perhaps the most prominent place in all of mission activity and recruitment efforts. It is now clearly evident that short-termers far outnumber career missionaries.

Most churches in sending countries strongly emphasize short terms as the logical starting point for missionary outreach and for attracting recruits, regardless of the age of those recruits. I have been able to see the pros and cons of short-term missions since I have watched this movement from its inception and seen the explosion of interest in this form of missionary work. Here are questions that need to be asked.

What do short terms do for the mission and the host missionary? Short-termers can often do a great job in helping to build a church, a home, a school or some other needed structure. This can be done without any knowledge of the local language or customs. Maintenance on older buildings is equally valuable.

Providing help to relieve the missionary of daily duties such as baby sitting or taking over some home projects can be greatly appreciated. Allowing missionaries to get away for needed rest or vacation can mean a lot.

Young people mixing with the youth of the local culture in a friendly way, even without the language skills, can open doors and help break down barriers. Older short-termers can often interact with professionals in their mutual disciplines, especially as English is such a universal language today. Most educated people in many countries have some skill in English and can communicate with the short-termer who does not know the local language.

Social-concern outreach to those in needy areas can be a great supplement to the mission. This is especially true for medical personnel such as general practitioners, internists, surgeons, ophthalmologists, dentists, plastic surgeons, podiatrists, nurses, etc. Equally important are the professional skills in almost any area of life and business. Financial help for local mission projects is often provided by short-term teams and is greatly appreciated by the mission.

But it also has to be known that short-term teams often work a major hardship for the missionary host. It takes much time and effort to plan for a team to visit. Hospitality, accommodations and meals must be provided. Interpreters must be available to work side by side with the foreigners. Interpretation must also be provided in public meetings where the short-termers preach and give testimonies. Often short-termers want to see the local sights and the career missionaries have to leave their work to serve as tour guides.

All of this can be a distraction for the missionary, taking him or her from a normal work schedule and responsibilities. Sometimes it happens that the missionary or the mission ends up with unexpected expenses that are not covered by the visitors.

Another question to ask is, "What do short terms do for the short-termers?" The greatest single value is what the trip does for those who go. Almost universally the short-termers receive a greatly altered appreciation and a new understanding of what mission work is about. God will often use this to lead some into long-term career missionary service. This is to be highly commended. It will also give those who get a renewed vision to support the work of missions through prayer and giving.

A new recognition of gifts that God has given, or a confirming of those gifts, will often be a by-product in the life of the short-termer. This will help with the sense of calling from God, either to confirm a new calling to missions or a confirmation that God's place for that person may not be overseas but rather in his or her homeland as a missions supporter.

One of the dangers for the short-termers is the idea that they will be making a major impact for fulfilling the Great Commission in the country to which they go. The idea that in a matter of weeks or months, or perhaps even a couple of years, one can learn the language adequately, assimilate the culture, learn the customs and thus plant the church is a disastrous fallacy.

An example of misguided training for short-termers came to my attention when a good friend told me the following. He was greatly excited because he and his youth group were being taken to an eastern European country for three weeks. He told me with great enthusiasm, "We will be doing evangelism, discipleship and follow up." Obviously, he had been told this by the leaders who were preparing them for the trip. But it is utterly preposterous that in three weeks in another culture and without the local language they could do those things. I was appalled that such an idea was being promulgated by supposedly responsible trainers for short terms. Even if this is not the norm, the fact that it can happen is dismaying.

Another question to ask is, "What do short terms do for the local church?" As it is for the individuals who go, the sending church will receive a new understanding of missions. There will be a renewed commitment to missions. There will be a recognition of the responsibility of the church to support those sent out from the church and also to support other ministries.

One of the dangers for the local church is to overemphasize short-term trips to the detriment of the ministry of long-term career missionaries. A sad fact in today's world is that many young career missionary candidates are struggling for longer and longer periods of time to raise the needed support to go overseas. At the same time, while many churches are investing thousands of dollars to send short-termers they are not responding to the needed support of career missionaries.

This is not an "either-or" situation but a "both-and." There are valuable reasons for supporting and participating in short-term outreach. But the career missionaries are still the ones who will plant the churches. They are the ones who immerse themselves in the language and culture and thus are far better equipped for establishing churches. They earn the respect and the love of the local believers who see that the career missionary is truly committed long term to them and to their churches.

It is my sincere hope that the church of Jesus Christ in sending countries will carefully evaluate and analyze all the dimensions of their investment in short-term outreach and that more and more short-termers will see this as a valuable stepping-stone to a long-term commitment to missions.

CHAPTER TWENTY FIVE
Please Don't Rob Me of That Blessing

They were a delightful couple with two small children. He had recently graduated from MIT as an engineer and they had now come to Colombia to work for an oil company. As committed Christians, Stu and Mimi Bengtson desired to serve the Lord in the marketplace.

Before moving to Colombia they had contacted the Latin America Mission to ask if LAM had any work in the city of Cartagena. They were referred to me, since I was responsible for the Colombia field of LAM and lived in Cartagena. They contacted me, telling me of their arrival and their interest in relating to the missionaries.

I remember meeting them in the lobby of the Hotel Caribe where they were staying temporarily after their arrival. I noticed this fine-looking couple across the lobby. It was a great pleasure to meet them and become acquainted.

They immediately became an active part of an English-speaking Sunday Bible study that I conducted among the expatriates who wanted to have a time of Sunday worship. Some of the people who attended were nominal church-going Christians. Others were committed Christians. A few were Colombians who spoke good English and wanted to be a part of this community.

Stu and Mimi became close friends. Our children played together with their children. They invited the missionaries to their home for such events as Thanksgiving or Christmas dinner. They were gladly serving the Lord as tentmakers.

One day Mimi asked me about our LAM Field Council. It was composed of eight to 10 missionaries who were leaders of our LAM ministries in Colombia. We usually met every two months for two days of review and strategic planning. Mimi asked, "Dave, where do you meet when your Field Council comes together?" I told her, "We meet in our office downtown."

My office was on the sixth floor of a building that was stifling hot most of the year. Mimi said, "You mean that you meet in that hot and humid office for two days? How can you stand it?" I replied that it never occurred to us to worry about this. Air conditioning was not even on our radar screen. None of the missionaries had it, nor did we ever think of it. This was normal life in the tropics.

Then Mimi said, "Dave, the next time your Field Council meets, please come and use our living room as we have such a cool house with air conditioning." I thanked Mimi and said we would gladly accept her invitation with the stipulation that we would go out for our meals for those two days.

"Oh no," Mimi replied, "I will serve your meals."

I rejected that part of her offer, insisting that while we would enjoy the luxury of using their air-conditioned living room for the meetings, we would plan for meals elsewhere. But she insisted. We argued back and forth on the issue. But then Mimi turned to me with tears in her eyes and said, "Dave, Stu and I came to Colombia to serve the Lord the best we can. We can't speak Spanish the way you can. We can't go out into the streets or into the rural and jungle areas where you go and witness to the people. But if I can do something to make your work a little easier and more comfortable, please don't rob me of that blessing."

I could not possibly turn down her kindness. So I accepted and the LAM Field Council began to enjoy the freshness of a comfortable air-conditioned home plus the delicious meals that Mimi served to us during our meetings.

Thirty years later, Stu and Mimi Bengtson were living in Miami, having completed their overseas assignment with the oil company. They became closely related to the LAM, whose administrative offices are located in Miami. Because of Stu's gifts and abilities as a businessman, he became a member of the Board of Trustees of LAM and served for a number of years as treasurer of the mission.

Stu and Mimi represent an entire category of so called tentmakers, that is, people who feel called of God to serve Him through their profession overseas. Because their salary comes from their company, they are self supporting, as the apostle Paul was through making tents. They do not need to raise support from churches or other sources, as full-time missionaries do.

This is an area where many fine Christians are making contributions to kingdom work without any expense to the churches in their homeland. It is also especially significant in areas of the world which are closed to missionary work. Their presence as Christians, even in a hostile society, can become leaven in demonstrating the gospel.

In the Bible class I taught to the expatriate community on Sundays in Cartagena, they decided on their own to take up a regular offering. We never even thought of such a thing, but to them this was their Sunday church, and an offering seemed to be a logical part of it. Because their salaries in business and the professions they represented were far higher than a missionary salary, we were constantly amazed at the size of the generous offerings. They would then pass these on to be used in the outreach ministry of the Latin America Mission. Over the years with the help of these offerings we were able to carry out many significant projects that otherwise could not have been done.

Because the ministry of Stu and Mimi was such an encouragement to us in Colombia, I find great joy in challenging professionals from all walks of life to consider using their profession as a means of strengthening the church and missionary work in other parts of the world.

CHAPTER TWENTY SIX
The Outreach of Agustin Ramos

He staggered into the church and flopped down on the back row. I was halfway through preaching a Sunday evening message in the Buen Pastor Church, a small church that Phyllis and I and our family were related to during our nine years in Cartagena. It was a typically hot and sultry evening.

After the service this man, whom I had never seen before, walked unsteadily up to the front to talk to me. The first thing he said to me was, "I have come here looking for the salvation of my soul." Because he was obviously inebriated, I almost did not take his statement seriously. My first thought was that he really did not know what he was saying.

Fortunately the Spirit of God did not permit me to dismiss him but to listen to what more he had to say. We sat down and he repeated his desire to find salvation for his soul. He told me that he was so frustrated and fed up with the lascivious and sinful life he had been leading that he could not take it any longer. He told the woman with whom he was living that he was going out that evening to look for the salvation of his soul and that he would not be back until he found it.

He had walked down the streets of Cartagena not knowing how to look for what he sought nor even what it was that he needed. As he shuffled along the dusty street he passed the open door of our small church and noticed that a "gringo" was preaching. Without knowing why, he slipped through the door to listen.

As we talked, he told me that his name was Agustin Ramos, and he told me more about the sort of life he had been living. He had a small jewelry stall in the local market where he repaired watches and did minor tasks with jewelry. However, most of his minimal income was spent on alcohol and women. He said that he was living, off and on, with fourteen women at the same time.

Presently he was living with a woman named Margot with whom he had five children. He probably didn't even know how many children he had scattered around with the other women with whom he consorted.

It was my privilege that night to explain the gospel to him and the life-giving and liberating power of Jesus Christ. He claimed to accept Christ even though I still had some reservations in my mind as to whether he really knew what he was saying, given his drunken condition.

Shortly after that, my family and I went to the U.S. on home assignment. I had no further contact with Agustin until we returned six months later. To my amazement I found that he had been faithfully attending the Buen Pastor Church. He had been witnessing to Margot and the children he had fathered. She soon indicated her desire to also receive Christ, as did some of the children.

Agustin decided that now he wanted to be legally married. So after the proper legal steps were completed, his marriage was arranged with Margot. I had the privilege of performing their wedding in the church with at least five of his children attending and participating.

One day there was a horrendous explosion in the central market of Cartagena. Some sticks of dynamite, which were hidden in the market and used illegally by local fishermen, had been ignited. Dozens of people were killed and at least 900 injured. Knowing that Agustin worked in the market, I immediately began to look for him. The central area of the market, where his stall had been located, was so completely demolished that it seemed questionable that anyone working in that area could have survived. So I began furiously searching for him in the local hospitals.

Finally, in the Santa Clara Hospital, I discovered Agustin in a bed in a large ward. I never would have recognized his face, which was totally bandaged. But his name was on a tag at the foot of the bed. He was alive but his prognosis was not hopeful. He was partially conscious and seemed to recognize that I had come to see him.

After some time, Agustin recovered from his injuries and was able to return to his work. God had more work for him to do because in his jewelry stall he had a partner named Raphael with whom Agustin shared the gospel. Soon Raphael accepted Christ as his Savior and became a true follower. Raphael then led his wife, Maria, to Christ, and their home became a Christian home.

Maria had a brother named Ramon Carmona. She witnessed to him and Ramon also accepted Christ. Ramon soon became an energetic and committed worker in the Buen Pastor Church. Before long he decided to go to seminary to prepare to serve the Lord on a full-time basis. So he enrolled in the Seminario Biblico de Colombian in Medellin and successfully completed his studies.

After his graduation from seminary, Ramon became a worker of the Asociacion de Iglesias Evangelicas del Carib (AIEC—the Association of Evangelical Churches of the Caribbean). He entered into a ministry of church planting which has been blessed of God in a remarkable way. He has planted six churches in the cities of Cartagena, Medellin and Bogota. The present church, which he planted in Cartagena, has 1200 members.

He was named as a facilitator for the churches of the AIEC. In this capacity he traveled extensively throughout Colombia encouraging and mentoring others in AIEC churches as well as many from other denominations. God blessed him with wonderful spiritual gifts. He has led numerous church-planting workshops and seminars on evangelism and discipleship.

Ramon married Gloria Paredes, daughter of don Mario Paredes, a leading layman of the Buen Pastor Church who was chairman of the elders of the church. Don Mario also became a church planter. He was active in helping to start and lead a growing church on the outskirts of Cartagena in a neighborhood called Blas de Lezo. That church started with a handful of street children whom Phyllis rounded up for a Sunday school and now has burgeoned into a large thriving church, which in turn has planted several other churches in Blas de Lezo.

Ramon Carmona was certainly not the only person responsible for this growth. Many other committed men and women participated in the amazing spread of the gospel. But at least part of that growth can be traced back to the night when a somewhat drunken Agustin Ramos went out of his house to seek the salvation of his soul. At that time there were seven evangelical churches in Cartagena. By 2009 that number had grown to 750 churches.

The Bible asks, *"Who despises the day of small things?"* (Zechariah 4:10 NIV)

Was it a "small thing" that Agustin Ramos staggered into the Buen Pastor Church one Sunday evening? I have often reflected on how close I came to not taking this man seriously because of his obvious condition. No, it was not a small thing that he entered that church, and it was not a small thing that the Holy Spirit prompted me to listen to him. Great things grew out of the small seed planted that night in the heart of a wanderer.

God is capable of taking the small and seemingly insignificant events in our lives and building them into something strong in the kingdom of God.

CHAPTER TWENTY SEVEN
Struggles of a Witch Doctor

As I stood in the humble thatched-roof home of Manuel Sena deep in the forest of Colombia, my spine tingled as he told me his story. His son, Francisco, and Francisco's wife were there, confirming the details of this disturbing tale. Along with them was Victor Landero, who had led Manuel to the Lord and participated in the story.

Manuel had been a witch doctor practicing a type of black magic. In his interaction with the spirit world he used many different fetishes for carrying out his magic. However, the Lord got control of Manuel's heart through the faithful witness of Victor Landero. On an Easter Sunday, in the remote village of Corozalito, I had the privilege of baptizing Manuel, along with a group of about thirty other new believers, in the small creek that flowed through that village.

After his conversion, Manuel had destroyed all of his fetishes and magic charms. He knew it was wrong to be involved in interaction with evil spirits, so he took that bold step. However, he secretly kept one small metal fetish. It was wrapped in a cloth, kept in a jar which was hidden in a box in the corner of his house.

Over a period of some months after his conversion he was rejoicing in his new faith. However, soon he began to be bothered by evil spirits who would molest him, primarily at night. They knew him from his previous life and they were not going to release him. Much as he tried to ignore these spirits, they continued to remind him that he had belonged to them.

Finally, in desperation, he took his son, Francisco, and they went to the home of Victor Landero, who lived about ten kilometers away in another part of the forest. Manuel told Victor about the problems he was experiencing with the demons. So Victor and Francisco laid hands on him and prayed earnestly for deliverance.

While they were praying, Manuel was suddenly thrown violently to the ground foaming at the mouth and then fell into a coma for a brief period. While in this coma Manuel began to speak out in a voice that was not his own. This is not uncommon with demon-possessed people, as was true in the New Testament. The voice revealed that he still kept that magic charm in his house. When he returned to his senses Victor asked him if this was true. Manuel confessed that it was.

So the next morning he asked Victor to come with him to his home and destroy that fetish for him. He was frightened to even touch it himself. Upon their arrival, Manuel's wife, who had been home alone the previous night while the men were praying in Victor's home, told them a hair-raising tale. She had no idea of what had been happening where they were.

At the same time that the men were praying at Victor's home, the dog in her house suddenly jumped up, began to bark furiously and tear around the house. She sensed a dark and terrifying presence that seemed to come out of the box that held Manuel's fetish. She jumped up on the bed and knelt there praying in great fear. The dog kept rushing around the room as she prayed. Finally the dog calmed down, the terrifying presence seemed to recede back into the box and she got back into bed with a sense of peace.

When the men arrived at the house in the morning, Manuel asked Victor to pull out the fetish and destroy it. He did not want to touch it himself. Victor went to the box, took out the jar and unwrapped the cloth where the metal charm had been kept. He found nothing but powder. The metal charm had totally disintegrated. The power of Christ had defeated the demonic powers that had held Manuel captive.

One of the lessons that came strongly to me at times like this was how easily we in the Western world can take evil spirit activity too lightly. Since we do not normally have much direct contact with the sort of things missionaries encounter, we tend to ignore this area. The devil is far stronger than we may realize, and his aim is primarily to destroy the work of God in the world.

Many other stories of this type can be told by missionaries who have experienced satanic opposition to their work. Whenever the gospel begins to penetrate an area for the first time, evil-spirit activity will follow almost immediately. This has been true throughout the history of the church and is still true today.

CHAPTER TWENTY EIGHT
Victor Landero: A Remarkable Man

Friends who know me well like to say that it is nearly impossible for Dave Howard to preach a sermon or teach a class or carry on a lengthy conversation without mentioning, in some form or another, Victor Landero. There is an element of truth in such a statement, and I gladly accept it.

Victor Landero was one of the most remarkable men I have ever met. I have written extensively about him in other books, especially *The Victor* (Fleming H. Revell 1979) and *Hammered as Gold* (Harper and Row 1969). Therefore, I will not repeat the story of his life here. Suffice it to say that he was an uneducated farmer from the backwoods of Colombia who became the most gifted personal evangelist I have ever known. His insights into the Word of God, his ability to explain the gospel to others and his quiet, humble demonstration of the fruit and gifts of the Holy Spirit in his life were second to none.

It was one of the greatest gifts of God to me to become acquainted with this man, to travel extensively with him in the forests or along jungle rivers in Colombia, and to learn from him, even though he thought of me as his teacher. I am convinced I learned far more from him than he did from me. He once referred to me as his best friend, and I am honored to know that he felt that way.

As the years passed and old age began to take its toll on him, I longed to see him once more before he entered his heavenly home. Finally, in June of 2008, the Lord gave me that opportunity.

After I had remarried, my wife Janet and I were able to visit Colombia, as I desired to show her the areas and some of the people with whom I had been privileged to work. We had visited Indonesia the previous year, where Janet had spent forty years with her first husband, so now it was time for her to see some of Colombia. Ubaldo Restan, a key leader among the churches of northern Colombia, kindly arranged to take us to visit Victor.

He drove us to the rural town of Planeta Rica, where Victor lived in a small house on a dusty road with his daughter, Anna, who cared for him. He was now 84 years old and suffering from dementia. His wife had preceded him to heaven years before.

As we drove up to the little house Victor was standing in the front window. I stepped up and greeted him, but there was no sign that he recognized me. Anna invited us in to sit with him in the front room. For the next hour I tried to talk with him, but it was evident that his clouded mind did not connect readily with me. I tried to reminisce about our old times together, and occasionally some reference would seem to strike a chord of memory for him.

Once his eyes suddenly brightened up, and he said two words with enthusiasm: *"Semana Santa!"* This means "Holy Week." I am sure he was remembering the many happy times he and I had enjoyed together in ministry during Easter Week. For the evangelicals of Colombia Easter Week is always the highlight of the year, the most important time in the ecclesiastical calendar. The story of the death and resurrection of Christ is a time for great worship and blessing. Victor almost always invited me to join him in the remote rural and jungle areas of Colombia during Holy Week. I am sure that was what he was recalling when he suddenly said *"Semana Santa."*

After an hour, which was mostly monologue on my part because of his inability to communicate, I told him that we would now be leaving. But before we left I wanted to pray with him. As I took his hand and started to pray, Victor began to weep. He wept profusely during my entire prayer holding tightly to my hand.

Then I said, "Don Victor, perhaps you would like to pray also?"

Immediately his head tilted upwards toward heaven, and he began to pray with fervor. He poured out his heart in praise and thanksgiving to God in totally lucid words and thoughts. During our entire hour together he had not been able to put together more than one or two words in talking to me. But the instant he began to talk to God, the words flowed easily, intelligently and fervently.

This was one of those rare moments when I wanted to take off my shoes, as I felt we were standing on holy ground. I look back on that visit with deep thankfulness to God who permitted me to have one more visit with this man of God who had so profoundly affected my life.

Several months after that visit the angel of the Lord quietly came and escorted Victor into the presence of the Lord whom he had loved and served so faithfully, When I get to heaven I expect to find him right up on the front row, and he will be wearing a shining crown of faithfulness.

Some of the blessings that God gives to missionaries, as well as to all believers serving Him, are the Victor Landeros whom God brings into our lives. They teach us and enrich us.

CHAPTER TWENTY NINE
My Hatred of David Howard

The man praying was sitting right next to me in a circle of about fifteen university students in a home in Bogotá, Colombia. He prayed, "Father, I want to ask forgiveness for my hatred of David Howard." I had never met him until that afternoon, so it was startling to hear such a prayer. I wondered what I had done to provoke his hatred of me. As he prayed, other students gathered around him, laying on hands and praying the same prayer. Now I was totally disoriented.

It was July 1973, and I had gone to Colombia to meet with one of the men whom I wanted to invite to speak at Urbana '73 to be held in December. I was staying in the home of LAM missionaries Jack and Mary Anne Voelkel who were working among university students, and that night they asked me to lead a Bible study with a group that met weekly in their home.

After I led the Bible study, we went into a time of prayer. The man to my right, who confessed his hatred for me, was the leader of the group. So his prayer was truly perplexing to me. As the others prayed with him I wondered what I had done to make this group hate me. Was it something I said during the Bible study? Was there a cultural mistake I had made that was serious enough to provoke hatred?

The majority of these students had come from the social background of that particular period in Colombia when Marxism had swept the student world. Most of them, while perhaps not card-carrying communists, had been greatly influenced by Marxism. Even though most of them were Christians, Marxism formed much of their thought patterns.

The man continued his prayer, saying something like this, "You know, Father, that because of the influence of communism in my life I had always been brought up to hate North Americans. Today, when I met David Howard for the first time, all of that pent-up hatred from my pre-Christian days welled up within me and poured out on him. Now I know that was wrong and I want to ask forgiveness."

This relaxed me somewhat, but it was still unsettling to realize that the majority of this group had actually hated me. After the time of prayer, the students gathered around me with hugs and words of appreciation. The "abrazo" was a common way of expressing love, even in those days when a hug was not as common as it is today. Then we began to sing scriptural choruses along with the guitar and a good time of fellowship was enjoyed as we sang together to the Lord.

Then they decided to sing some protest songs, heavily weighted songs of political protest against the social and economic evils of the day. Suddenly somebody said, "Let's sing 'Subdesarrollado' for Dave; just for him." They had me sit down while they gathered around me in a semi-circle to sing the song, accompanied by some lively dancing.

"Subdesarrollado" means "underdeveloped." This was a long ballad about the underdeveloped countries of Latin America and how they had been exploited by the foreigners. It started out with the Spanish conquistadors and continued through the French and British pirates. Then the song turned into a vicious and prolonged attack on the colossus to the north—the despised "Yanquis." It went on and on with vitriolic hatred for all that North America had done and represented to the underdeveloped countries of the south.

Now I was totally disoriented. How was I to respond to this when just a few minutes earlier they had prayed for forgiveness of their hatred for me? Now they were singing a song of hatred toward my country. While I am woefully aware of the sins of my country and do not defend everything that the United States has done over the centuries in Latin America, I still love my country and am aware that God is the one who made me a North American. How was I to react to this?

When they finished singing, they asked me, "How did you like that?" Now, what was I to say? The truth was that I did not like the words of the song. And I found it hard to put together their previous prayers for forgiveness with the specific singing of a song of deep hatred of my country. But I did like the tune. So, I responded, "I liked it."

I knew immediately that this was a lie. But in my mind I justified what I said because I liked the tune. So the evening ended and we went our separate ways. I returned to the U.S. to continue the preparations for Urbana '73 that was coming up.

All through the next months, in the overwhelming busyness of preparing for that convention, I tried to forget that incident, especially the fact that I had lied to those students. But this kept gnawing at my conscience and I knew that I had to do something about it.

Finally in November I took a half-day off for prayer and meditation on what I must do. After much thought, with fear and trepidation, I sat down and wrote a letter to my friends in Bogotá, addressing it to the leader of the group who had started the whole situation with his prayer asking forgiveness for his hatred of me.

My letter said two things. First, I confessed that I had wronged them by lying to them. It was not true that I had liked their song, even though I had enjoyed the tune. I said that I owed them an apology and I asked their forgiveness for my untruthfulness. Then I said that I felt that they also owed me an apology. Immediately after having asked forgiveness for their hatred of me, they had sung specifically to me a song of hatred against my country. How could they honestly put those two things together?

When I mailed the letter, I feared that those students, most of whom had been heavily influenced by Marxism, might react strongly against me. But I felt that I owed this to them, to be honest both in confession of my failure to them as well as pointing out their failure to me.

A few days later I received a response from the leader. This is a paraphrase, but in his letter he said, "David, you are the first person to put his finger on my besetting sin. In all my pre-Christian years, when I was taught to hate North Americans, I carried that hatred in my heart. Even after becoming a follower of Christ, I still had that hatred in my heart, which is what poured out on you that day. Therefore, I want to thank you for your honesty. I also want to ask your forgiveness for that entire situation." Then he closed by saying, "David, I love you. I want you to know that I love you."

About three days later I received a second letter from him which said, "Just in case you missed the point of my last letter, I want to reemphasize this and assure you that I love you and am grateful for what you have done for me." I was deeply grateful and gratified.

At Urbana '73 I always made it a point to mingle with the students in the afternoon to observe how they were responding to the convention and to listen to their thoughts. One afternoon, as I was wandering through the huge armory where the mission board displays were held, a young woman headed toward me, smiling in a pleasant way as though maybe I might know her. After a few minutes I asked her where she was from. She told me she was from Colombia, so I switched to Spanish. I asked her if she was a student there and which university. She replied that it was the National University in Bogotá.

By this time her smile was bigger than ever so I asked her if she had been in the group the past July when I met with the IVCF students. She replied, "Yes, I was there and those students paid my way to Urbana representing them and especially to say 'Thank you' to you for what you have done for us. Your letter touched a sorely troubling area of our lives, and we are thankful for your honesty in pointing out to us our besetting sin." Then she reached into her handbag and pulled out a small package and handed it to me. She said, "This is our gift of appreciation to you."

I opened the package to find a hand tooled brass plate with Colombian Indian designs. Today, that brass plate is on the wall above my desk. It is a reminder to me to always share honestly about my own sinfulness even as I point out the failure of others.

The student who prayed the first prayer that night is Jorge Atiencia, a highly respected evangelical leader in Colombia and throughout Latin America. He is a brilliant man, a gifted Bible teacher and discipler of others. He is a long-time member of the Latin America Mission, a good friend of mine and was the daily Bible teacher at Urbana '96. I thank God for his life and ministry.

Two things stand out in my mind as I reflect on the lessons of that experience. First, when we are involved in the work of the Lord we never know when some unexpected opposition may arise. I was taken totally by surprise with the hatred expressed by those students as they prayed for forgiveness. The fact that such hatred had existed, even that very evening, was disconcerting to me. But I had to realize that as a missionary of the gospel such hatred should not be surprising. It was my responsibility to respond properly to this situation, which I failed to do at first.

Second, I am deeply thankful today that I responded to the Lord's urging to write to my friends in Bogotá. I had to confess my sin to them but also be bold enough to bring to their attention how they had wronged me. Had I not done so, the nagging uncomfortable feelings of that evening would still be with me. The close friendship I now have with that leader, and others, might never have developed. I would have missed a deep lesson for myself about obeying the promptings of God in my life.

SECTION THREE

Observations of A World Missiologist

CHAPTER THIRTY
The Many and the One

It was my privilege to direct the IVCF student missions conventions known as Urbana during the 1970s. As I sat on the platform looking out at thousands of students gathered in the large assembly hall at the University of Illinois, my heart was moved with compassion toward them. That assembly hall will handle 17,000 to 18,000 students, and it was jammed. As I looked up at those large crowds I thought of the tremendous potential for the work of the gospel around the world should all of those students give themselves unreservedly to Jesus Christ for outreach with the gospel. I had reason to sense something of the same feelings that Jesus must have had when He saw the multitudes.

As I study the life of Jesus Christ, it is evident that He spent His ministry both reaching out to multitudes and also sitting down with individuals. We read that, "When he saw the crowds, he had compassion on them, because they were harassed and helpless, like sheep without a shepherd" (Matthew 9:36 NIV). This phrase is repeated several times in the Gospels where He was moved by the multitudes and spent time teaching them.

We also read how He sat down frequently with an individual and showed deep concern for that person. Examples of this, of course, are Nicodemus in John 3, the Samaritan woman in John 4, the rich young ruler and others mentioned in other parts of the Gospels.

Years later, after I had directed several Urbana conventions, I was back in that same assembly hall under totally different circumstances. This time I was not sitting on the platform looking up into the stands. Rather, I was one of the spectators in the stands looking down at the floor of the assembly hall. There was no platform there on that occasion; rather, there were six wrestling mats laid out on the floor. The event was the Illinois State High School Wrestling Championships. The boys who were competing for the championship had to qualify first by winning their way through a district tournament in another part of the state. If they won through that tournament they qualified to wrestle in the sectional tournament. If they won in the sectional tournament they then qualified to compete in the state championships at the University of Illinois in Urbana.

The reason I was there was that my son Michael was one of those wrestlers. He had won through both district and sectional tournaments and qualified to compete for the state championship.

As I sat in the stands looking down on those mats, I was constantly listening for an announcement that would go something like this: "The next match to be wrestled on mat number two in the 132-pound weight class will be Michael Howard of Wheaton North High School." Whenever I heard that announcement I immediately lost sight of all the thousands of other people in that large assembly hall. For the next few minutes I was concentrating totally and exclusively on one person; that is, my own flesh and blood. As Michael wrestled the next match, I was with him in every movement. My palms were sweating and my knuckles were white as I agonized with him through every match. He did well in that tournament. He won seven or eight matches. He finally lost by one point and thus did not win the state championship; however, he did exceptionally well and I was proud of him.

As I thought about my different experiences in that assembly hall at the University of Illinois, Urbana, I could see the difference of when Jesus was moved with compassion by large multitudes but also took the time to sit down with individuals who needed Him. I had the same sort of feelings. Looking up from the platform at the IVCF Missionary Convention was a moving experience. Looking down from the stands on one single person who was competing at a wrestling match was a totally different but equally moving experience.

I have often thought of the comparison of those two perspectives both in the life of Christ and in my own personal life. As I have worked especially with young people over the years on behalf of missions, I liked to challenge them with the multitudes of unreached people around the world; but I also liked to challenge them with the need of one single individual with whom they have an opportunity for ministry.

On another occasion I had a similar experience where thinking about large crowds or one individual was very meaningful to me. I was in the city of Bangkok in Thailand. One evening I walked through the lobby of the hotel where I was staying and noticed that a large crowd was gathering around the main entrance to the hotel. I soon noticed that large black limousines were pulling up in front

The Many and the One

of the hotel. Men and women from different parts of the world were stepping out and entering in to go up to the main ballroom of the hotel.

I waited and watched as diplomats from many different areas of the world were heading up into the main ballroom. Finally one more big black limousine pulled up, the prime minister of Thailand stepped out, and with him was Deng Xiaoping, the premier of the Peoples Republic of China.

I had seen his picture many times in newspapers, magazines, and on TV. Every time I had seen his picture, he was to me nothing more than a symbol of the largest country in the world. To me he was a symbol of oppression, of persecution of the church of Jesus Christ, of difficulties with other countries in the world, and various other aspects of life. Suddenly, however, this man in person was walking right toward me.

I was impressed with the fact that here was a man who represented the largest multitude of people in the world; however, he himself was an individual human being. He was not a symbol, he was not at that point the leader of an oppressive regime; rather, he was one man, one member of the human race for whom Jesus had died. My mind swirled with thoughts about what I was seeing. Instead of seeing a symbol of the multitudes I was seeing one human being.

As a result of this experience I asked God to help me to see both the multitudes for which Jesus was moved with compassion and also each individual whom He loved and for whom He had died. When I see the great needs of multitudes of people around the world I never want to lose sight of the one individual whom God might put directly in front of me.

CHAPTER THIRTY ONE
Urbana—Threats and Prayers

"If I have to shed my blood to get this convention closed down, I will shed my blood. This missions convention is irrelevant. You need to get with the real issues of the day and get away from this irrelevant business of foreign missions. I will do whatever is necessary either to get you to change or I will get this closed down."

This was a threat from a Christian student at Urbana '70. He was representing a group of radical students at the IVCF triennial missions convention which was challenging students with God's call to world evangelism. It was at the height of the "counterculture" movement of the late 1960s and early 1970s. These students were publishing a daily underground newspaper condemning the convention and handing it out on the streets of Urbana, doing all they could to undermine the convention.

It was a generation that was protesting almost everything: government, education, church, missions and society in general. The protests took various forms ranging from mild verbal protests to peaceful or noisy marches to sit-ins to violently taking over university buildings and offices and even to blowing up buildings. Tangles with the campus and local law-enforcement officers leading to confrontations with the National Guard, became the order of the day. It reached its peak when the National Guard, responding to taunts and threats from radical students, shot four students at Kent State University in Ohio.

That period of our history has been analyzed and dissected by sociologists, historians, politicians and many others. But Urbana '70 came at the heart of these protests. Thus, among the 12,000 students at that convention, there were some who were caught up in the mindset of the radicals of that generation. They wanted us to totally change the focus and purposes of the convention, to turn from biblical foundations for God's plan for world evangelization and focus on such issues as war, poverty, economic injustice, racism, etc. While IVCF recognized the importance of these issues, we felt that they must be placed into the broader scope of God's concern for the needs of the human race including salvation, making disciples and building the church of Jesus Christ throughout the world.

It was not easy to deal with these protests. The campus security of the University of Illinois had to be out in force. The National Guard had to be alerted to possible upheavals. And we at IVCF had to be ready to stand our ground on why we held such a convention and why its focus was primarily on the needs of the world in terms of building His church.

In spite of such opposition, which was indeed very real, the Lord intervened and kept the convention on track. The security forces of the University of Illinois did their job by their evident presence on campus. And the Lord held in check the threats of radical students who wished to disrupt and change the entire program. Paul Little and the rest of the staff stood firm.

The response of these students was not what we had wished for. Some were strongly negative. But others responded positively to the call of God to world missions. The majority seemed rather neutral in terms of outward response.

However, over the years since that convention I have traveled extensively all over the world visiting 70 or 80 countries. Almost everywhere I have been, I have had the joy of hearing missionaries and national church leaders tell me that they attended Urbana '70 or subsequent ones in 1973 and 1976, and that Urbana was used of God to call them into his service.

Urbana '70 was under the leadership of Paul Little, who was a veteran IVCF staff member with unusual gifts for evangelism and relating to the current culture. I served as his assistant, having just returned from fifteen years as a missionary in Latin America. My culture shock upon returning to my homeland was far greater than any culture shock I encountered when first going to the mission field, so I was grateful to learn under such a godly and gifted man as Paul Little. IVCF then passed leadership to me to prepare and direct Urbana '73 and '76.

To direct this huge convention is a gigantic task in itself. It takes three years to work out the program that will be relevant to the students of that generation. We needed to find the right speakers and workshop leaders and make the necessary preparations for recruiting. Logistics such as housing, feeding, transportation, assembly hall arrangements and classrooms and all the other details were required for the success of the convention.

By the end of those three years of intensive work, both preparing and then directing the operation, I was utterly drained. Even though it was exciting, exhilarating and gratifying, I was physically, emotionally and spiritually exhausted. In December, just a couple of weeks before the convention was to begin, I woke up one morning so thoroughly drained that I could not drag myself out of bed. I called my administrative assistant to tell her that I would not be in the office that day. Then I lay listlessly in bed trying to pray but scarcely having the energy to do even that.

After several hours, I called one of my special prayer partners, Frank Murray. He was a pastor with more than fifty years of pastoral experience in a church in Massachusetts. His major emphasis in all those years was a ministry of prayer. Seldom have I heard anyone pray with such authority and power. When he prayed, one was lifted right into the presence of the Almighty. I explained to him how I felt.

First he gave me some words of encouragement; then he spoke to me from Daniel chapter 10. Daniel had just experienced 21 days of intense spiritual warfare. He said, "I had no strength left, my face turned deathly pale and I was helpless...My strength is gone and I can hardly breathe" (Daniel 10:8, 17 NIV). That was exactly how I felt.

Then the text tells us that Michael the Archangel sent a special messenger to Daniel who touched him and set him trembling on his hands and knees and touched Daniel's lips, giving him strength, and said, "'Do not be afraid, O man highly esteemed...Peace. Be strong now; be strong.'" And Daniel responded, "When he spoke to me, I was strengthened" (Daniel 10:19 NIV).

Then Frank Murray began to pray, saying, "Now, Lord, there is Dave Howard out in Madison, Wisconsin. He has been working intensely to prepare for this great convention to challenge thousands of students for missions. The devil does not want this to happen. He has attacked Dave Howard and wants to immobilize him so that he cannot adequately direct that great gathering. Dave is exhausted and needs a special touch from you. So, Lord, I ask you to send that same angel you sent to Daniel to touch him and restore him and put him on his feet. Send that angel now to Dave Howard."

I am not a mystic and do not have experiences of this type very often, but I can say that as Frank prayed I suddenly felt strength flowing back into my body from my feet right on up through every part of my body and through my head. Physically, I became totally revived.

When Frank finished praying, he said to me, "OK, Dave, get up and go back to work." And that is exactly what I did. I was fully restored physically, emotionally and spiritually. I had all the energy I needed to carry out the responsibilities of the convention director. I have seldom had such a dramatic and immediate answer to prayer. It was unmistakably clear that God had used Frank Murray and an angel from heaven to revive me and give me all I needed to do the job.

As I reflect on that crucial experience in my life, I am overwhelmingly thankful for the earnest prayer support of Frank Murray. I shudder to think of how I might have weathered that satanic attack on my body and soul without his powerful prayers on my behalf.

I also wonder if I am giving that kind of intense prayer support to others who look to me for such help. I have friends all over the world for whom I pray. I do not have the gifts of Frank Murray but I do know the promises of God about prayer. It is my honest desire to be faithful in prayer for missionaries and other Christian workers relying on the manifold grace of God in their lives.

CHAPTER THIRTY TWO
Sold Out to Satan

My experience with demonic activity was not limited to Colombia. About the time that we returned to the U.S. to work with InterVarsity Christian Fellowship in the late 1960s, witchcraft, Ouija boards and similar activities were becoming a rage among college students. Witchcraft shops were springing up near college campuses.

Somehow the word got around IVCF circles that I was an expert in this area. This was not true, but I soon became the "in-house" authority in dealing with such matters. Increasingly I was being invited to speak to student groups on the topic of witchcraft, demonism and related subjects.

One night I spoke at the University of Wisconsin in Whitewater on this topic. As I headed for the classroom designated for this meeting, I found the hallways jammed with scores of students. The classroom was overflowing and students were streaming into the building from all over campus. It soon became evident that they would have to find another location. No other classroom or auditorium was either large enough or available, so they decided to use the grandstands outside at the university track. No sound system had been planned for this open-air venue.

It was a spring evening, so weather was not a problem. Therefore I had to stand out on the track with hundreds of students (calculated at 800 or more) sitting in the stands or on the grass near the track. So I gave my talk, shouting at the top of my lungs. This showed me just how interested students were in this subject about the devil and his tactics.

Another time, I was to speak on the same topic at the University of Wisconsin at Madison. The meeting had been announced around campus, so again we had a large crowd. Afterwards a number of students came up to discuss this with me. I noticed that one male student and a young woman (apparently his girlfriend) were standing quietly to the side. After most of the students had finished with their questions, this couple sidled up to me with some hesitation and asked, "Is it ever possible for a person who has sold himself body, soul and spirit to the devil to be delivered?"

I noticed that he was quite nervous His lips were tight and trembling, his hands were clenched, with white knuckles. While he did not say that he was talking about himself, it was apparent to me that he was. Several of the mature Christian students noticed that this was a deep and serious case so they urged me to go into a side room and they would stay and pray for me. I asked one of them to come into the room with us and pray right there while we were talking. We went into a room, and the next hour-and-a-half was one of the most terrifying and tension-filled times that I have ever experienced.

Gerald (not his real name) told me that he was a member of a coven of witches who met regularly to practice their witchcraft. He showed me a scar and told me that he had sold himself to the devil with a blood covenant. The blood from where he had cut himself filled a golden vial. This vial was then passed around and the other members of the coven drank his blood. This, he said, was a covenant with Satan that could never be broken.

He told me stories of using a goat's head in their rituals and of many other procedures as part of their worship of Satan. He said that at midnight he prayed to Lucifer, who would appear to him. He said that if other members of the coven knew that he was telling me these things he would be killed. As he spoke, he was perspiring, shaking, clenching his fists, tightening his lips and showing other signs of nervousness.

Finally he asked me, "Is it ever possible for me to be delivered from this blood covenant that I have made with Satan? I belong to Satan, but I want to know if I can be freed."

I knew the answer perfectly well. I had been a Christian since the age of ten and had been brought up in a strong home and church. The answer was, of course he could be delivered. But he asked, "Is it possible to do that right now?" Suddenly my own faith was placed squarely on the table. Did I really believe that God could deliver Gerald right now? I knew that God could deliver him, but would God deliver him right now?

Taking my cue from Nehemiah when the king asked him a pointed question, "I prayed to the God of heaven, and I answered" (Nehemiah 2:4b–5a). I told Gerald that the only thing more powerful than his blood covenant with Satan was the blood of Jesus Christ, which could deliver him and cleanse him from all sin. Gerald then asked, "Can you do this for me?" I answered, "No, you have to do it yourself."

"What do I have to do?" he asked. I told him, "You must recognize and confess your sin, asking God to forgive and deliver you." Gerald protested, "But I don't know how to pray." I said, "You just told me that you prayed to Lucifer every night. Now you must pray to God. I want you to pray first, telling God of your sins and your desire to have your blood covenant with Satan broken. Then I will pray with you."

So Gerald began to pray, and almost instantly he was thrown to the floor grabbing his stomach and crying out in agony and writhing on the floor. I stepped over and laid my hands on him, claiming the blood of Jesus Christ to defeat the devil in this terrible battle. I do not recall how long this struggle lasted; it seemed like ages.

Soon Gerald relaxed, rose to his feet and, with a big and genuine smile on his face, turned to his girlfriend and said, "Wow! This is real. This really happened." I knew he had been forgiven and delivered, it showed in his face and body language. Then I turned to his girlfriend and asked, "What about you? What is your relationship to Jesus Christ?" She replied in a forlorn way, "I don't know." So I asked her, "Would you like to get right with Jesus Christ tonight?" She affirmed that she would, so I had the privilege of leading her to the Lord right there.

After this long struggle in the side room, we went out to join the other IVCF students who were still praying for us. I asked Gerald to tell them what had just taken place in his life. He did so in clear and unmistakable words. The students rejoiced, hugged him and shouted, "Welcome to the family."

Then Gerald asked, "But what am I to do when Lucifer comes to see me at midnight?" I told him to rebuke Lucifer, claim the blood of Jesus Christ and pray to God for protection. The IVCF students joined in and said, "We will pray for you all night tonight and surround you with prayer."

One student said, "Here is my phone number. Any time—day or night—that you are troubled again by Lucifer, you call me. I will then call these other friends and we will all back you up in prayer."

For the next few weeks, Gerald had no further trouble with the devil. But the attacks resumed some weeks later and he called for help, which was readily given by the IVCF students. Later that year Gerald asked me to perform the wedding of him and his girlfriend, which I was honored and delighted to do. One of the IVCF students who served as his best man gave them a wedding gift which was a scholarship to attend Urbana '73, which I had the privilege of directing.

Once again Satan was defeated and Jesus Christ was glorified.

It is extremely dangerous to enter into spiritual warfare alone. In a struggle with satanic forces, we desperately need the support and help of other believers. We dare not underestimate the power of the devil. The archangel Michael did not enter alone into combat with Satan. Jude reminds us of this by saying, "But even the archangel Michael, when he was disputing with the devil about the body of Moses, did not dare to bring a slanderous accusation against him, but said, 'The Lord rebuke you!'" (Jude 9, NIV). Thus Michael was invoking the help of the Lord.

When we are involved in spiritual warfare with the forces of our enemy, it is vitally important that we do the same in seeking the help of others in prayer,

CHAPTER THREE
The Influence of a Faithful Man

It was December 26, 1976. The next day Urbana '76 would open at the University of Illinois. Seventeen thousand students, from across North America as well as other countries, would be there. That evening, about 500 IVCF staff was gathered for an opening banquet and final orientation and instructions about their responsibilities during the coming five days of the convention.

Dr. John W. Alexander, president of IVCF, was presiding. After welcoming the staff and making some important announcements and preliminary remarks, he said to all in that room, "As of this moment I am placing everyone in this room, including myself, under the total direction of David Howard for the next five days."

This was Dr. Alexander's management philosophy. He believed in delegation. He wanted to delegate down the line of administration every decision that could be made at a lower level. But he also held firmly to the belief that some decisions could only be made up the management ladder. Those on the upper levels had to accept the responsibility of making those decisions, no matter how difficult they might be.

General Dwight D. Eisenhower showed this same kind of leadership when he insisted that a decision that could be made by a lieutenant should not be made by a captain, or what could be decided by a captain should not be decided by a major, and on up the line through colonels and generals. This meant that as commander-in-chief of this operation, he had to make the most agonizing decision of all. It was his responsibility to give the final command for the invasion of Europe in spite of the surrounding dangers and possible disasters. While he insisted that his subordinates pass on down the line decisions that could be made at a lower level, they must accept the heavy responsibility of making those decisions that must be made at their level.

Eisenhower enacted this management philosophy when he was appointed to plan, organize and carry out the greatest military operation in history—the invasion of Normandy in June 1944. He accepted the fact that some decisions could be made only by him as Supreme Commander of the Allied forces. In his book *Crusade in Europe*, he writes poignantly about the agony he went through on the night before D-Day, when he had to make the final call to start the invasion. The weather was questionable. It could destroy the landing crafts. No other day would work for the next 28 days because of the tides based on the moon. He had a million men poised in England, ready to carry out the invasion. If they didn't go that day, what could he do with them for 28 more days? How would he keep the Germans off guard by keeping the location of the invasion from them?

Eisenhower accepted the fact that this decision was his—and his alone—and he made it. The rest is history.

In the same way, Dr. Alexander was superb in following this philosophy of management for himself and for his entire staff. It was a delight to work under the leadership of such a man.

I recall seeing some missionaries who fail to follow this principle by not delegating to others, especially to national coworkers, the responsibility that should have been theirs. One time I attended a church being planted by a missionary in another country. The missionary led the singing with his guitar, made the announcements, led in prayer, took the offering and preached the sermon. That church could not, and did not, prosper under such leadership.

The "other side of the coin" sometimes would come into play also. When I was Field Director of my mission in Colombia, we had a missionary who was constantly delving into other people's responsibility, telling them how to run their work. I finally had to call her into my office and tell her that eight different people had complained to me that she was trying to run their work for them. She found this hard to believe this and wanted to know who the eight people were. I refused to give their names, as I wanted her to face the big picture and not get into trying to justify herself.

The principle of delegation can be used in wonderful ways to strengthen and develop God-given gifts in others. I thank God for men like John Alexander who did this for me.

Earlier he was insistent in his invitation to me to serve with InterVarsity. My wife and I were serving as missionaries in Latin America and fully expected to spend the rest of our lives there. But then, when I was speaking at Urbana '67, Dr. Alexander approached me to say that IVCF needed a new Missions staff member and that he and his colleagues believed that I was the person to take that position. I told him that I could not accept.

But he asked me if I would pray about it for a while. So after we returned to Latin America I did pray about it for about two months. But the Lord gave me no freedom to make such a change. So I wrote to Dr. Alexander and told him that I could not accept. He wrote back asking me to pray about it a little longer. So I agreed, but after two more months of prayer, I still felt no such leading from the Lord. Therefore I turned down the invitation a second time.

Dr. Alexander wrote back, saying, "I am convinced that you are the man to take this position. Please pray a little longer." His persistence was incredible. I was finding myself torn. I wanted to stay in Latin America, which we dearly loved, but those were the days of campus unrest with negativism toward the church and missions. The thought of getting back into the student world to challenge them with what the Word of God says about our responsibility to the world was attractive to me.

One day I wrote in my journal, "Lord, if this call from IVCF is really from you, and you want me to return to the U.S. to be Missions staff member of IVCF, please have Dr. Alexander write back one more time and *leave the door open*." That meant he would have to write to me a fourth time. If he did that, and left the door open, I would take this as from the Lord for His leading.

Shortly after writing this request in my journal, I received another letter from Dr. Alexander. He wrote, "Apparently the Lord is not leading you in our direction so I will not be bothering you further. However, if in the meantime you get any green light from the Lord, may I *leave the door open?*"

There have been few times in my life when I felt as though I had heard an audible voice from the Lord. This was one of those times. I almost felt as though the Lord had shouted in my ear that now He wanted me to leave Latin America, return to the U.S. and accept the position of Missions staff member and Director of the Urbana conventions. For the next ten years I worked with university students under Dr. Alexander and his staff.

CHAPTER THIRTY FOUR
Just Before I Jumped

In the Indian city of Hyderabad it was my privilege to meet Sadhu Chellappa, a former Hindu scholar and now a remarkable Christian evangelist. As I stayed in his home for several days, I was able to hear his life story, which to me is most remarkable.

Sadhu Chellappa explained to me that as a former Hindu scholar he studied the Sanskrit writings of the Hindus. He explained that most people who know Hindu writings have read the Bhagavad-Gita. These are writings written sometime in the period of about AD 900. However, there are some more ancient Hindu writings which were written largely in Sanskrit and therefore are not available to the average reader. These are known as the Vedas. As a Sanskrit scholar, Sadhu Chellappa was able to read these ancient writings which went back as far as 1000 BC, or 3,000 years ago.

Sadhu Chellappa said that he had a great emptiness in his heart. He realized that he was seeking the true God but seemed unable to find Him. In the ancient writings of the Vedas he found intriguing references to someone whom he did not know but for whom he sought. He found in the writings known as Ashtothra Namavali various references to someone known as God, the Son of God. These references are the following: "The one who is called the son of God," "the one who is born of the Holy Spirit," "the one who is born of a virgin," "the one who is sacrificed on a trishul, like a tree," "the one who has five wounds on the body," "the one who gave his flesh willingly," "the one who has victory over death."

Sadhu Chellappa became intrigued over who this person might be. He sought diligently for years, trying to find who this would be and how this might relate to the emptiness in his own heart. However, he was unable to find the answer to his deep questions. Finally he gave up the search and became an atheist. He lived a profligate life and finally came to the verge of suicide. In his desperation he decided to commit suicide by getting on a train, waiting until it was running at full speed, then stepping up to the back platform and throwing himself off the train.

The time came when he was ready to jump. At the last moment before jumping he heard a voice. When he related this story to me, I interrupted and said, "You mean a voice from heaven?" He replied to me, "No, I heard a human voice. It was someone preaching through a loudspeaker in the open air in a small village as the train went speeding by." The voice he heard said the following: "He who conceals his sins does not prosper, but whoever confesses and renounces them finds mercy" (Proverbs 28:13 NIV).

When he heard those words Sadhu said to himself, "That's what I'm looking for! I need mercy. Perhaps that person preaching can tell me how to find it." Therefore, instead of jumping off the train, he stayed on to the next station, got off and then took a train back to the village where he had heard this voice over the loudspeaker. When he got off the train, the man who was preaching in the open air was still there. Sadhu Chellappa went over, heard the gospel and received Jesus Christ into his life. He said this was the answer to his long-time search.

The result was that today Sadhu Chellappa travels all over India preaching the gospel. He is fluent in seven or eight languages and dialects of India. He begins his message quoting from the Vedas and then going on to say, "Now let me tell you who that man is that the Vedas speak about." And of course at that point he preaches Jesus Christ.

As he told me this story I was overwhelmed with how this illustrates the power of the Word of God. The simple, straightforward message of Scripture caught Chellappa's ears and heart, and he became the effective evangelist that he is today. I realized anew how God's Word will not return void. I have seen again and again in my ministry that the proclaimed Word of God has power.

CHAPTER THIRTY FIVE
Trends in Missions

He was sitting at a desk in the Missionary Research Library of Union Theological Seminary in New York City. His desk was piled high with books and documents spread out before him, as he seemed to be concentrating diligently on research. His name was Denton Lotz. I had met him only once and did not know him well.

I was in the library to do research for some lectures I was preparing on the influence of students on the mission outreach of the church. I was very much a fledgling researcher on this topic and did not have anywhere near the resources I needed to do the job adequately. Gordon Conwell Theological Seminary had asked me to lecture for a week on that topic and I hardly knew where to begin. But I decided that the Missionary Research Library would be a logical place to start.

As I looked across the room at Denton Lotz, he seemed so engrossed in his study that I decided not to bother speaking to him. After all, we had met only once and scarcely knew each other, so why bother him? Today I shudder as I think about how close I came to not greeting him.

Fortunately, I decided to go over and say hello. We engaged in small talk for a moment or two and then I asked what he was doing. He was working on his doctoral dissertation for the University of Hamburg on the topic of the watchword of the great Student Volunteer Movement (SVM). That famous watchword was "The Evangelization of the World in this Generation."

Denton Lotz had in front of him all the available documentation on this topic that could be found probably anywhere in the world. He had delved into musty and long-forgotten documents hidden in the most remote archives for the history of that great watchword which had challenged thousands of students to go into foreign missions outreach.

When I told him what I was working on, he pointed me to a large variety of materials that were precisely what I needed and which I likely never would have discovered without his help. In the light of subsequent events, this meeting was a "divine appointment" that God knew I needed.

Denton Lotz showed me how the SVM was founded in 1886 in Northfield, Massachusetts, at the conference grounds sponsored by D.L. Moody. However, one enormously significant aspect of that movement took place in 1920 at the quadrennial missions conference which SVM held for students. The original founders of SVM were visionary students who became great missionary statesmen, such as John R. Mott, Robert Wilder and others. By 1920, 34 years after the founding of SVM, the younger generation of students was rebelling against the older leadership.

Their rebellion can be summarized as: "Your generation has taken us through a bloody and useless world war (World War I). You failed to solve the great social problems of the world with your emphasis on such things as Bible study, evangelism and foreign missions. We are going to change that. Rather than emphasizing foreign missions, we will concentrate on the great social issues of today such as war, race relations, economic injustice, poverty and imperialism. We will rid the world of these evils."

At the 1920 SVM convention, held in Des Moines, Iowa, 6,890 students attended. Of those who were there, 2,783 signed missionary decision cards and 637 of them sailed for overseas missions during that year. However, because of that change of focus, by the mid 1930s the missions emphasis of SVM had been almost totally lost. In 1934, only 38 students from SVM sailed for overseas missions; in 1938 there were only 25 signed missionary decisions cards; in 1940, only 465 attended the quadrennial convention. In spite of this disastrous decline in mission outreach, SVM did not return to its original missions focus.

Therefore, in 1936 a group of Christian students, attending a Bible conference at Ben Lippen conference grounds in North Carolina, decided that, since they had been unsuccessful in reviving the SVM to its original focus, they would start their own movement to challenge students for missions. With the encouragement of Dr. Robert McQuilken, founder and president of Columbia Bible College (now Columbia International University), they formed the "Student Foreign Missions Fellowship" (SFMF), and that movement merged with InterVarsity Christian fellowship in 1945.

Years later, as we were preparing for Urbana '70, students were at the height of the counterculture and protest movements. We came under great pressure to change the focus of the program at Urbana. The issues of Vietnam, racial tensions, poverty, war and other issues brought pressure to drop the "irrelevant issues" of Bible study, evangelism and world missions. Students threatened riots on the floor of the convention.

As these threats escalated, my mind went back to my divine appointment with Denton Lotz the year before. The similarity to the SVM position shook me. The SVM was founded in 1886. Thirty-four years later there was that student revolt at the convention in Des Moines. Then SFMF was formed in 1936, later to combine with IVCF. Exactly 34 years later we were facing the same kind of revolt at Urbana '70.

When we saw the similarity between the two movements and the pressures being faced, we realized that were we to concede and change our focus, we faced exactly the same scenario that led to the demise of SVM. This put iron in our bones and caused us to resist the strong pressures to change the focus of the convention.

Today I thank the Lord for that divine appointment with Denton Lotz who provided me with that relevant and important material that led to our seeing how the missions thrust of our day could suffer the same fate as the SVM.

Fortunately, there were major changes in student attitudes in the later 1970s and subsequent generations. Students were responding in a positive way to the call of God to missionary service. As I travel around the world I frequently meet missionaries and national leaders who thank me for what God did in their lives during Urbana '73 and '76 in calling them into missionary service. I had seen firsthand that "In his heart a man plans his course, but the Lord determines his steps," (Proverbs 16:9 NIV) God had led me to speak to Denton Lotz, and he helped me to see the direction of SVM. Denton Lotz received his PhD, became a missionary and seminary professor in Europe, and later became the leader of his denomination's international missions.

More than 34 years have passed since that crisis during our preparations for Urbana 70 when students pressured us to follow the same path that 34 years earlier led to the failure and death of the SVM. We may be at the same crossroads today.

I am painfully aware that "what goes around comes around." The strong emphasis today for the church and missions to be involved in social and political concerns is biblical and correct. However, just as former movements have lost their bearings because of an unbalanced focus, the danger is always present for such an imbalance to creep in. The problem of the SVM was that they made it an "either/or" situation. Either they were to follow the founders' principles of evangelism and world missions or they were to focus on social and political issues of the time. They chose the latter and thus lost their bearings and eventually died.

May God grant that the church and missions of today maintain a truly biblical balance between the spiritual, social, and political needs of the world.

CHAPTER THIRTY SIX
Those Bible Notes

His questions went on and on. "How do you know that God exists? How can you be sure that the Bible is the Word of God? Why do you say that Jesus is the only way to God? What happens to those who never heard of Jesus?"

We were at an IVCF weekend conference in the mountains of California. Most of the students were eager and open to studying the Word of God and applying it to their lives. However, Milt was marching to a different drummer. He asked far more questions in less time than most students with whom I have been associated. Several of us on IVCF staff met with him individually and tried to help him work through the questions in his mind and heart. We tried to take him seriously, even though at times it almost seemed that he was enjoying trying to make us squirm. His questions were tough and we were not very successful in answering them.

One afternoon I spent about three hours with Milt listening to his questions and trying to get him to see what the Word of God had to say about the problems he was bringing up. I had my Bible in hand and would show passages to him, asking him to read what the Word said. But he kept being distracted by something that was in my Bible.

When I was majoring in Bible at Wheaton College, I took several courses in archeology from Dr. Joseph Free, an outstanding biblical scholar and archeologist. One of the requirements that Dr. Free had in each of his courses was that we were to make notes in our Bibles of archeological finds that confirmed the Scriptures. We were to insert the notes either in the margins or on small slips of paper on which we wrote out the essential points of the archeological find and then insert the slips into our Bibles at the appropriate passages. Since I had taken several courses from Dr. Free, my Bible was full of such notes.

As I showed Milt passages of Scripture that I wanted him to read, he kept being distracted by all those notes. He would ask, "What is that note that you have there?" Or, "Let me see what you have written in the margin." But I wanted him to read not what I had written but what God himself had said. So I told him, "Just ignore that for the moment. I want you to read what God Himself has written."

As we finished our time together, Milt asked, "May I borrow your Bible for a while?" I was glad to let him have it thinking he wanted to read what God said for himself.

Milt returned my Bible to me and when our weekend conference ended, we did not have much hope that there had been any change in Milt's life. Personally, I felt somewhat defeated in my feeble efforts to be of help to him. I didn't hear about him again for many years.

Ten years later I was speaking at a conference in New England directed by Peter Haile, regional director of IVCF for that area. Peter's wife, Jane, was also present. She had been part of that conference in California ten years earlier before she married Peter. One day Jane and I were reminiscing about our experiences with IVCF when she asked, "Do you remember that conference we had in the mountains of California ten years ago?" Of course I remembered, so she added, "Do you remember that student who had so many questions?" I remembered.

Jane then told me, "That student somehow got hold of a Bible that was full of archaeological notes that proved the authenticity of the Bible and repeatedly confirmed biblical passages. He read those notes and also the Bible earnestly, and the Lord used that to bring him to Christ. He decided that if the Bible truly was the authoritative Word of God, then he had to submit himself to Jesus Christ, the central figure of the Bible. So he accepted Christ."

When Jane Haile related that story to me, my heart leaped with joy. It was a classic example of what God promises so clearly in His Word: "As the rain and the snow come down from heaven, and do not return to it without watering the earth and making it bud and flourish, so that it yields seed for the sower and bread for the eater, so is my word that goes out from my mouth; It will not return to me empty, but will accomplish what I desire" (Isaiah 55: 10–11 NIV).

This promise of the power of God's Word is one of the greatest sources of encouragement for any Christian worker. There will be times when we wonder if there has been any result of giving out the Word of God. My hours with Milt were surely one of those times. But the Word did not return void even though I never knew until years later what the Word of God was doing in Milt's heart.

CHAPTER THIRTY SEVEN
Arrested!

Caesar Molebatsi, growing up as a young man in South Africa, hated all white people. He was on the receiving end of how the Afrikaners treated the blacks under Apartheid. One day he was walking down the road when a white man in a car deliberately chased him off the road and ran over his leg. His leg was so severely mangled that it had to be amputated. When I knew Caesar he walked with a prosthesis, giving him a distinct limp. He swore that he would never speak to a white man again.

But a missionary in South Africa named Allen Lutz, whom I had known at Wheaton College as a fellow student, heard about Caesar, so he decided to visit him. He went to Caesar's house and knocked on the door. When Caesar came to the door Allen said, "Caesar, I hear that you hate white men and will never speak to one again. I understand that. This is O.K. with me. You don't have to speak to me, but I want you to know that I love you and I am your friend." Whereupon Allen sat down on Caesar's front porch and stayed there quietly for some time.

The next week he returned and followed the same plan. He told Caesar that he loved him and wanted to be his friend, and then sat quietly on the porch for a while.

Caesar himself related this story to me. I asked him how long this went on. He said that Allen kept this up for weeks.

Finally Caesar began to realize that Allen was sincere and really meant what he said. Slowly and with hesitation Caesar began to talk to Allen, who eventually led him to Christ. He then joined Allen in a holistic outreach which Allen was leading among the needy people of Soweto. The first time I met Caesar he was a student in the Graduate School of Wheaton College studying for an MA to better prepare for ministry to his own people.

Allen's love, so evident to Caesar, broke down the racial barriers and freed Caesar to demonstrate that same love in his community. Years later, when I was having lunch with Caesar in his home in South West Township on the outskirts of Johannesburg, I was arrested.

Caesar was living in the area where black South Africans who worked in Johannesburg had to live back in the days of Apartheid. At least two million blacks lived there and commuted daily in and out of Johannesburg since they were forbidden to live in the city.

Caesar had invited me to visit him and to see the outreach work he was doing in evangelism and discipleship, feeding the hungry, teaching reading, giving medical advice and help and providing various other holistic ministries. I had known him previously and was now speaking in several places in South Africa sponsored by InterVarsity.

As we were sitting at lunch, a van full of South African police pulled up in front of the house. Caesar went out to see what they wanted. He came back and said, "Dave, they want to talk to you." So I went out to respond.

At that time white people were not welcome in Soweto, so my presence had prompted some interest. The police questioned me about why I was there. They wanted to see my passport and they asked such things as, "Who are you?" "Where are you from?" "Why are you here?" "What are you doing here?"

Finally they seemed satisfied that I was no threat to anyone, and they left.

Half an hour later a large truck filled with SADF (South African Defense Forces) personnel pulled up. They were all heavily armed. Three of them, carrying large rifles, came right into the house. They turned to me immediately and then the same process of questioning took place.

After a rather short time of questioning they said, "Sir, you must come with us now to police headquarters."

Caesar immediately said, "If you are going to take him to the police station, I will go along, as he is my guest. I will be glad to drive him there."

The SADF officer agreed, but he placed two heavily armed soldiers in the back seat of Caesar's car as we drove to the police station. Upon arrival he and I were escorted up to the third floor of the police headquarters where several officers were standing around their white commander who was sitting at a desk. He had a dossier open in front of him and immediately began to question me with the same questions I had already answered twice.

He kept asking about my passport, which I had given to him. "What kind of a passport is this?" I explained that it was a legitimate passport issued by the State Department of the USA.

But since he kept zeroing in with this question, I finally said, "Well, I do have another passport."

"So why do you have another one?"

"Because I am visiting other countries in Africa also," I replied. "If a visa from South Africa appears in my passport, the other countries will not allow me to enter. So the State Department allows me to travel with two passports—one exclusively for South Africa and one for the other countries."

With great sarcasm and anger he said, "Yeah, they all think we have leprosy, don't they? I'm sick of your disgusting double standards."

At that point I nearly lost control of my tongue and wanted to blurt out, "Who in the world has worse double standards than you white people of South Africa?" But I bit my tongue and decided to keep quiet.

Then he suddenly turned on Caesar and said, "And who are you?"

"I am Rev. Molebatsi."

One of the other officers standing there peered closely and suspiciously at Caesar and slowly said, "Are you by any chance Caesar Molebatsi?"

"I am," he replied without hesitation.

"Weeell, we have a whole barrel full of files on you," the officer sneered.

Caesar said, "I'm sure you do. That's fine. Bring them all out and let's talk about them."

At that point the commanding officer looked at his watch and said, "I'm fed up with you guys. It's time to quit. I'm going to lock you up, and I'm going home."

Caesar said, "Sir, if you are going to lock us up, you must call General Coetze first, as he is a friend of mine. He has told me that if I ever get in trouble with the SADF, have them call me."

General Coetze was the commander of the entire SADF in that area and he knew that Caesar was a good man doing a fine work in Soweto. This unnerved the officer at police headquarters. At that point he turned to me and spit out, "You get out." So I was escorted downstairs and out the door to the street.

At this point, for the first time, I began to get worried. I had no idea what they might do to Caesar. He had told me that every day when he left his house, his wife never knew if she would ever see him again. He said that he was under attack constantly from the black radicals on the left as well as from the white supremacists on the right.

He said, "The radicals could put a necklace on me anytime." A "necklace" was an automobile tire filled with gasoline, placed around the neck of a victim and set on fire. "Or the white radicals could dispose of me in a wide variety of ways, and I would never be seen again."

I spent the next half hour out on the street praying for Caesar. Finally he emerged and seemed quite relaxed. He said with a smile, "You can't let these fellows intimidate you. They grill me, and I talk to them in Afrikaans. This always disorients them as they never expect a black to speak their language as all blacks hate the language of the Afrikaners. So I do that on purpose, and they don't know what to make of me."

As he and I returned to his house Caesar said to me, "I feel like a drowning man ten miles from shore with nothing to grab hold of. Unless people like you can understand what we are facing on a daily basis here, I have no hope. But I know the power of the Lord to sustain me."

This incident was all the more amazing to me when I reflected on who Caesar had once been.

CHAPTER THIRTY EIGHT
The Bombshell of Lausanne '74

In 1969, Dr. Ralph Winter of the Fuller School of World Missions in Pasadena, California, wrote a book entitled *The Twenty-five Unbelievable Years*. He traced the amazing growth of the missions movement from the close of World War II in 1945 up to the date of his writing. He showed how the church had exploded exponentially around the globe and how the message of the gospel was now penetrating every area of the world.

It was an encouraging and well-documented statement which gave hope and optimism to the missions movement. In fact, it was so encouraging that mission leaders were beginning to feel that we were very close to fulfilling the Great Commission of Jesus Christ. His last command was to "preach the good news to all creation" (Mark 16:15 NIV), and "to make disciples of all nations" (Matt. 28:19 NIV). Was it not true now that the church existed in almost every nation of the world? If this was so, and apparently it was, then was not the great commission completed? Dr. Winter's optimistic summary of the twenty-five years from 1945–1969 gave great hope to the church.

During that period several world congresses on evangelism and missions added to the optimism that was so pervasive. One of them was held in Wheaton, Illinois, in 1966, and the other in Berlin, Germany, also in 1966. Encouraging statements came out of those congresses.

Thus by the early 1970s this feeling of nearly completing the Great Commission was picking up speed. Therefore a group of key evangelical leaders began to consider another congress on world evangelization which would study the next steps for the church as it moved into the future. With Billy Graham as Chair, Bishop Jack Dain as Chair of the Executive Committee and Leighton Ford as Program Chair, these leaders undertook the planning for this congress.

Thus in July 1974, the International Congress on World Evangelization convened in Lausanne, Switzerland, with 2,430 participants and 570 observers from 150 countries. Billy Graham served as chairman; Donald Hoke, veteran missionary to Japan, served as director of the Congress; and Leighton Ford was program chairman.

The Congress was divided into many workshops and seminars as well as plenary sessions. Current issues in the world and in missions were discussed in great depth. Eleven major papers had been circulated to the participants in advance soliciting their response. The plenary sessions were built on seven "Biblical Foundation Papers" and five "Issue Strategy Papers," plus other major addresses, three panel discussions and two multimedia programs.

As the participants and observers gathered, there was a spirit of excited expectation and optimism. Nothing on this scale among evangelicals had ever been attempted before, and we who were participants all anticipated a great movement of the Spirit of God as we looked toward fulfilling the Great Commission.

Then, suddenly, in the plenary sessions a huge "bombshell" was dropped. Dr. Donald McGavran and Dr. Ralph Winter shook us up by claiming that, in spite of all our optimism about fulfilling the Great Commission, more than half the world's population had never been faced adequately with the claims of Jesus Christ. They used the figure of 2.7 billion people who had never been given the opportunity to accept or reject Jesus Christ. They claimed that there were approximately 16,500 "hidden people groups" in the world without the gospel.

The term "hidden peoples" became the accepted terminology for a while. However, it was not long before missiologists began to recognize that to call, for example, the one billion inhabitants of China "hidden" was inaccurate. How can you hide nearly one fourth of the world's population? Therefore, the new terminology of "unreached peoples" came into use and replaced "hidden peoples."

The impact of what we were seeing was unmistakable. A sudden shift of focus took place. Up to that time missions had emphasized geography. This was both inevitable and correct. When the gospel was first reaching out from Europe and then North America, geography had to be the target—to get the gospel to every nation.

Thus many of the missions founded in the latter half of the nineteenth century and the first decades of the twentieth century used geography in their names. For example, there was the China Inland Mission, the Sudan Interior Mission, the Africa Inland Mission, the West Indies Mission, the Central

American Mission, the Oriental Missionary Society and the Latin America Mission, to name just a few.

At Lausanne '74 however, Drs. McGravan and Winter pointed out to us in graphic ways that missions must now change its focus from geography to people groups. The unreached peoples of the world are scattered throughout every geographic region. This led to intensive study on how to define a "people group." It seems that there are endless possible definitions depending on how detailed we want to be. A people group may be a large linguistic group in one geographic area or even scattered over several regions. Or a people group might be defined as narrowly as the Cambodian taxi drivers of Los Angeles or the Sudanese refugees in a housing project in Nairobi. While definitions may vary, they usually revolve around the linguistic, ethnic, geographic or professional affinity that a certain group of people shares in common.

The bombshell that Drs. McGavran and Winter dropped onto the world of missions in 1974 was revolutionary. It required an entirely new way of thinking about missions. Strategic planning had to be refocused from geography to the unreached peoples of the world.

It is significant that many of the mission organizations that had geography in their names have now changed their official names. For example, China Inland Mission is now OMF, Sudan Interior Mission is now SIM International, Central American Mission is now CAM International, Far Eastern Gospel Crusade is now SEND International. In some cases there were mergers with other missions which extended the sphere of missionary activity to other regions of the world. For example, the former Sudan Interior Mission, because of several mergers with other missions, now works in Latin America and Asia as well.

Another significant contribution of the Lausanne '74 Congress was the formation of the "Lausanne Covenant." Throughout the Congress, a carefully chosen committee listened to what was evolving in the workshops, seminars and plenary sessions. Under the steady hand, theological acumen and skillful use of the English language of Dr. John R.W. Stott, a covenant was drafted and presented to the Congress for ratification.

The covenant discussed such issues as: the relationship of evangelism and social concern; unity, diversity and cooperation among Christians; the uniqueness of Christ; the validity of missions; the work of the Holy Spirit in evangelism; religious liberty; and the relationship of the gospel to culture. By the end of the Congress, an overwhelming majority of the participants had signed the covenant, thereby agreeing to follow its precepts in their personal lives and share its truths with their home churches and constituencies.

The Lausanne Covenant has continued to have an ongoing and in-depth impact on missions and the church of Jesus Christ. It has been translated into dozens of languages and has formed the basis of the statement of faith for a wide variety of Christian organizations.

Lausanne '74 caused a paradigm shift of monumental importance and altered the course of missions from that point on. Probably few of us at the time realized how earthshaking this was. But we can see today that we were participating in an historic milestone that would alter irrevocably the strategies and direction of missions for decades to come.

CHAPTER THIRTY NINE
The Elephant and the Crocodile

Years ago it was my privilege to spend time in the land of Zambia, whose southern border is the Zambezi River dividing the country from Zimbabwe. One of the great cataracts, Victoria Falls, is located on that river. Having heard of this spectacular falls for years, I wanted to see it while I was in Zambia. So a trip was arranged to go there.

I was not disappointed. All I'd heard or imagined about that great falls turned out to be true. The Africans have a wonderful onomatopoetic name for the falls. They call it "musiotumna," which means, I was told, "the smoke that thunders." From a distance of several miles one can see the mist rising high from the rushing water that cascades over the precipice. This looks like smoke. The roar of the cascading water sounds like thunder, thus the name that the Africans have given to it.

A statue of David Livingstone, the great British missionary and world-famous explorer who was the first white man to see the falls, stands in the forest as he looks at the falls. He named it Victoria Falls in honor of his English queen. The Africans laughingly say, "You white people think that David Livingstone discovered the falls. We knew they were there all along."

While standing by the river some distance above the falls, we talked with a boatman who had a commercial launch in which he carried passengers up and down the river. He told us that if we had been there three days earlier we could have witnessed an interesting event that he saw. He described it to us.

He said a herd of elephants was crossing the river from one side to the other. Some parts of the river at that point are too deep for the younger elephants to get through safely. So the large bull elephants lined up side by side and formed a dam with their bodies. This held back enough water so that the water became more shallow. Thus the younger elephants were able to cross over safely.

However, as the bull elephants were standing there forming the dam, a huge crocodile came along under water and clamped on to the leg of one of the elephants. The elephant calmly reached down with his trunk, grabbed the upper jaw of the crocodile, ripped it off his leg and held the whole body of the crocodile up in the air. Another elephant saw that his colleague had been attacked. So he came over, grabbed the lower portion of the crocodile's jaw, and between the two of them ripped the crocodile in two right down the middle. They tossed the torn body back into the water and formed the dam again until the entire herd was across on the other side.

I saw two illustrations in this. The larger bull elephants were helping the weaker smaller elephants to cross the river. We need to be there to help the weaker among us. The second illustration I saw in this was that elephants do not live in the water, crocodiles do. Thus the crocodile sees the elephant as an invader of his territory and attacks. The elephant is forced into a struggle to survive. But one elephant can't destroy a crocodile by himself. He needs the help of another to come over and help him and thus destroy the attacker.

In mission outreach, the missionary is invading territory long held by the enemy, Satan. The enemy does not give up his territory without a fight, and missionaries will face severe attacks. This is especially true where the gospel has not yet penetrated. When this happens, there needs to be cooperation with the strong helping the weak. The new "babes in Christ" in that area will need the full cooperation of those who have known the Lord longer and can provide help and protection to the younger ones.

At the same time, it can be expected that the missionaries themselves will be attacked. One person cannot fight the enemy alone. It takes the help of others, just as it took two elephants to destroy the crocodile.

The question each of us must ask ourselves is "What am I doing to support my colleagues working in difficult areas who are under attack by the enemy? Are my prayers, affirmations and my support of all kinds participating in the struggle to wrench that territory from Satan?"

CHAPTER FORTY
Another Man in His Cell

During the years when Communism was in control in Eastern Europe I had the privilege of preaching in a Baptist church in Sofia, the capital city of Bulgaria. The pastor, Ivan Angelof, was not present when I spoke because he was preaching in an outlying village that night. His son, Theodore, served as my interpreter.

After the service, as Theodore drove me back to my hotel, I asked him about his father, as I had heard that Ivan Angelof had spent significant time in prison. Theodore confirmed that this was true.

"Yes," he said, "When the Communists took over Bulgaria they imprisoned many of the pastors and tried hard to break their faith. Father spent ten years in prison. I was eight years old when he went to prison, and I scarcely saw him again until I was eighteen because I was allowed only once or twice to make a short visit to him."

Theodore then gave me the following story.

"The prison officials tried everything they could to break Ivan and make him recant his faith. But Ivan began every day by saying, 'Lord, I am your prisoner. You placed me here. Now give me the grace just for today to live as a prisoner of Jesus Christ should live.' Since he began every day with this prayer, God granted his request and gave him the grace to hold up under crushing persecution.

"One time they starved Ivan for 15 days, giving him only water. At the end of that time he was very weak. They dragged him out into the courtyard of the prison and gave him a terrible beating. They knocked him down with clubs, beat him with rifle butts and kicked him around mercilessly. In his weakened state from the starving, he was almost unconscious.

"Finally the prison guards told him to get back into his cell. He could not even stand up, so he crawled painfully across the prison courtyard. In his cell the only item he had was a blanket, so he was looking forward to curling up in the blanket and nursing his wounds.

"As he crawled into the cell he saw that another man was wrapped in his blanket. His heart sank in despair. He knew that one of the tricks used in Communist prisons was to beat a man within an inch of his life hoping he might turn delirious. Then in his delirium he might give away information that could then be used against him, his family, his church or others. An informant would be placed in the cell with him to get the information which he might let out.

"When Ivan saw this other man he assumed he was an informant placed there to draw out information. In his despair he fell back against the wall of the cell and lay there weeping. Finally in his weakness he called out audibly to the Lord, saying, 'Lord, I just can't take it anymore.'

"Whereupon the other man spoke up and said, 'Ivan, what do you mean that you can't take it anymore?'

"Ivan thought that now he must be doubly careful, realizing that in his weakness he might say something he should not say. So he simply repeated aloud, 'I just can't take it anymore.'

"The man in the blanket spoke up and said, 'Ivan, have you forgotten that Jesus is with you right now?'

"Ivan looked up and saw that the man had disappeared. No one was in the blanket. He realized that Jesus Himself had come to be with him in the most desperate time of his life. In his delight he jumped up and began dancing round the cell singing and praising the Lord even though he had not been able to walk a few minutes before. He spent the rest of the night dancing, singing and praising God.

"The next morning the guard who had beaten him so viciously saw him and said, 'Who gave you something to eat?'

"Ivan replied, 'I haven't had anything to eat.'

"'Well, why do you look so different this morning?'

"'Because my Lord was with me last night.'

"'Oh, is that so? Well, where is your Lord now?'

"Ivan opened his shirt, pointed to his heart, and said, 'He's right here.'

"Whereupon the guard pulled out his pistol, pointed it right at Ivan's chest and said, 'Then I am going to shoot you and your Lord right now.'

"Ivan replied, 'Go ahead, if you wish, because if you shoot me now, I will just go to be with my Lord.'

"The baffled guard put his pistol back into the holster and said, 'You sure can't fool these Christians.'"

Then Theodore went on to tell me that one night when he was a teenager his mother called him and his sister together. She explained that she did not know what was going on in the prison that night but she had a strong sense that they needed to pray earnestly for their father. Before praying she took out the big family Bible saying that she wanted to read some Scripture before praying. She did not know where she wanted to read.

The Bible fell open to Isaiah 51 and her eye fell instantly on verses 14–15, which almost jumped off the page at her. She read, *"The cowering prisoners will soon be set free; they will not die in their dungeon, nor will they lack bread. For I am the LORD your God..."* (NIV).

As Theodore recounted this story to me he said, "I don't know if Isaiah knew to whom he was writing those words, but as far as I am concerned, he was writing them for us."

Shortly after this Ivan was released. The Communists apparently decided that it was hopeless to try to make him deny his faith. He continued to serve the Lord faithfully up to his death some years later.

Although I have never been beaten for my faith, other believers have been, and in some places today Christians are still being beaten. I pray for them when I hear their stories and pray for myself to be faithful no matter what may come to me. I know many believers who pray each day, "Give me grace just for today."

CHAPTER FORTY ONE
I Was Saved in a Bar

"I was saved in a bar and I was the owner of the bar."

The man who said that was Francisco Pitty, a new student at the Latin American Biblical Seminary in Costa Rica where I was a professor. At the start of the school year we would have the new students give their testimonies as to how God had worked in their lives and why they had come to seminary to prepare to serve the Lord.

Francisco Pitty was older than the average student. He had three children by the time he came to seminary and was probably in his mid-thirties. In the testimony meeting in the beginning of the school year he stood up and spoke the words mentioned above. Then he went on to explain. "I had a bar in Panama, where I lived, and every day, and especially every night, I would be selling drinks to the men who came in to carouse in my bar. One night one of the men had a few extra drinks and became a little high and happy. He started to preach like an evangelist in the middle of the bar. This encouraged the other men in the bar to urge him on and to get him to preach more forcefully. Finally he stood up on a table in the middle of my bar and began to preach very enthusiastically, waving his arms and quoting Scripture. He had obviously had contact with the gospel and he knew some Scripture. As this man was quoting the Bible, it was a straightforward message of the gospel of Jesus Christ. Even though those words were being preached in a mocking way through the mouth of a drunkard, it was still the unadulterated Word of God.

"I heard those words and they struck deeply into my heart." As the writer of Hebrews tells us, "The Word of God is living and active. Sharper than any double-edged sword, it penetrates even to dividing soul and spirit, joints and marrow; it judges the thoughts and attitudes of the heart" (Hebrews 4:12 NIV).

Francisco went on to say that on that evening, under the conviction of the Word of God, he went home, fell to his knees and received Jesus Christ into his heart. At the time of his testimony he told me that he was now coming to the seminary in Costa Rica to learn more about the Word of God so that he could become a pastor. After graduating from seminary in Costa Rica he returned to Panama where he carried on an outstanding ministry as a leading preacher. This illustrates to me the straightforward power of the Word of God quite apart from the one who proclaims it.

CHAPTER FORTY TWO
The Danger of Twisting Scripture

Some years ago, in a two-week period, I observed how easy it is to take one verse of Scripture and trumpet it to support a viewpoint. Here is what I saw and heard.

I was at a conference ground where an evangelist was preaching on Acts 3. He spoke of how Peter and John went up to the temple to pray and encountered the man crippled from birth. The poor beggar asked them for money. Peter's answer was clear: "Silver or gold I do not have, but what I have I give to you. In the name of Jesus Christ of Nazareth, walk" (Acts 3:6 NIV).

With forthright emphasis the speaker hammered home the point that physical or social elements such as money or healing were not Peter's primary concern. Rather, Peter was concerned for the man's salvation. Hence his emphasis on "In the name of Jesus Christ of Nazareth…" The speaker went on to say how we must not be sidetracked into social matters when the salvation of souls is our primary concern.

The following week I was at a second conference where a respected mission leader preached on the same passage. His major thrust was that in our evangelistic efforts, which are a vital part of our gospel ministry, we dare not neglect the physical needs of those around us. He developed this by showing that Peter was an evangelist at heart. This is evident on every page in the early chapters of the Book of Acts.

Peter realized that spiritual needs are not the only needs of a human being. Here was a poor man who had no money because his physical limitations prohibited him from normal work. Therefore, from the perspective of the beggar, his greatest need was physical. Consequently, Peter took action to solve the physical problem. But he put it in the context of "Jesus Christ of Nazareth" so that the man would come to see how Jesus was able to meet his need. Obviously the crippled man made this connection because "he went with them into the temple courts, walking and jumping and praising God" (Acts 3:8 NIV).

Peter took advantage of the sudden stir in the temple that the healing of this man caused. He turned to the crowds and preached one of his most powerful sermons, glorifying God and calling the people to repentance (Acts 3:12–26). This resulted in Peter and John ending up in jail overnight, which led to further investigation by the authorities that opened the door for another great sermon by Peter that's recorded in chapter 4.

Thus we see Peter as a well-balanced evangelist. He understood that the simple message of salvation through Jesus Christ is the heart of the gospel. But concern for physical and social needs is interwoven in the gospel and cannot be neglected. This is seen clearly in the answer of Jesus Christ to the question of which is the greatest command. He said, "Love the Lord your God with all your heart and with all your soul and with all your mind. This is the first and greatest commandment. And the second is like it: Love your neighbor as yourself. All the Law and the Prophets hang on these two commandments" (Matthew 22:37–40, NIV).

Those two incidents within a two-week period came a full decade before the Lausanne Conference of 1974 where our eyes were being opened again to the fullness of the gospel message. Having grown up in the more "Fundamentalist" wing of Christendom, I tended in my mind to agree with the first speaker. I was uneasy about evangelism being mixed with social concerns.

But as I saw how these two men, both committed and well-respected Christians, were using the same passage of Scripture to prove an opposite viewpoint, I began to realize how careful we must be in our interpretation of God's Word. Within a few years I found myself to be wholeheartedly in the camp of those who believe that we cannot separate evangelism and social concerns but that both are the heart and soul of the gospel.

I believe it is correct to say that this is seldom an issue today among committed Christians. Nearly all who claim to be evangelical Christians will fully support the holistic view of the gospel. But it is important that we "take heed how we build" in our use of Scripture to support our viewpoint. Both evangelism and social concerns are part of the gospel that is to be proclaimed in all the world. To neglect either is to minimize the fullness of the true gospel message and thus even to falsify it.

CHAPTER FORTY THREE
A Timely Phone Call

"Mr. Howard, there is a phone call for you."

A deaconess at the Fellowship Deaconry in Elburn, Illinois, interrupted our meeting. The International Council of the World Evangelical Fellowship (WEF) was holding an extraordinary meeting called by the Chairman, Dr. Tokumboh Adeyemo. An emergency had come up. The phone call turned out to be perhaps the most significant call I have ever received.

When I took over responsibilities as International Director of WEF, with evangelical alliances or fellowships in more than 120 countries of the world and which is today known as the World Evangelical Alliance (WEA), we were having severe struggles. A loss of administrative leadership had prompted the call to me to serve as International Director. But almost immediately things went from bad to worse in the area of finances. We were struggling day by day to make ends meet. Fund raising is not one of my gifts, nor have I ever enjoyed it or felt called to do much of it. However, as head of WEF, this became part of my job description.

After four years of sweating this out, feeling that I did not have the full support of the council and recognizing my own limitations in the area of fund raising, I decided to resign. My resignation was genuine and not just a plea for help. I had no idea where I would go next but I felt that I did not have what it takes to lead a loosely organized worldwide fellowship such as WEF. My resignation spurred the council to call this meeting.

On the first day, the Chairman asked me to put my resignation on hold for the time being until we could discern what God's will for the future might be. I agreed to do so. Dr. Adeyemo led us in a memorable Bible study plus extended times of prayer for God's direction.

By the second day, the mood was depressing. We all saw the urgent needs in WEF, but no easy solution became evident. Most of the members seemed discouraged, feeling helpless. One member was especially pessimistic, and most of his participation was couched in negative terms. That day he proposed that we simply fold up WEF, which had been in existence since 1846, including a special renewal of the movement in 1951. While this seemed to make some sense, there was no general feeling that this was God's leading. There was even the specific mention that some of the Lausanne Movement leaders such as Brian Stiller, Ramez Attallah and Clive Calver had shown no interest in WEF.

Then came that phone call. Brian Stiller, who was the general secretary of the Evangelical Fellowship of Canada and a member of WEF, was on the line. "Dave," he said, "I heard that you have resigned. You can't do that," he exploded. Then he went on to lecture me for the next ten or fifteen minutes. He said, "You cannot resign from WEF. Your leadership is exactly what is needed. The worldwide evangelical church needs what WEF offers in developing unity and cooperation among the churches. The Lausanne Committee is fulfilling a special need in evangelization, but WEF has the goal of spiritual unity among the churches. We need WEF."

Then, to my surprise he started mentioning names. He said, "I have talked to Ramez Attallah (of Egypt) and Clive Calver (general secretary of the Evangelical Alliance of Great Britain) and Ajith Fernado, (head of Youth For Christ in Sri Lanka), and they heartily agree with me. They feel that WEF is crucial to the church today and that you are the man to give the leadership that WEF needs. So you cannot resign." The fact that he mentioned some of the same names that were mentioned earlier by the pessimistic member of the Council was especially significant.

I returned to our meeting and said, "You are not going to believe what I am about to tell you." Then I recounted Brian's call, what he said, and especially that he mentioned the names of some of the Lausanne leaders. This utterly amazed the Council members who were sinking lower and lower into despair. The timing of that phone call, which could have come only from the Lord, changed the atmosphere in that room almost instantly. The Council, instead of continuing to talk about how we could best disband WEF, began to start creative planning for the forward movement of WEF.

As this whole new and positive mindset took hold, one of the major decisions was to move WEF headquarters from Wheaton, Illinois, to Singapore. It would put WEF in the heart of the non-Western world. It would demonstrate that

WEF was international in its scope and purpose. Singapore is the crossroads of Asia and thus of much of the world.

One of the members of the WEF Council, John Langlois, from Guernsey in the Channel Islands of the United Kingdom, was both a lawyer and a Member of Parliament. He had participated in countless meetings over the years. But when he saw what was happening as a result of Brian Stiller's phone call, he said, "In all my years of public service I have never seen such a dramatic turnaround in a meeting as we have experienced. It was so clearly the hand of the Lord that we could not ignore it. We can only praise God for His clear leading."

A year later we moved the international offices of WEF to Singapore. My wife and I spent the next five and a half years there experiencing some of the most fruitful years of our ministry together. What one phone call did for WEF and thus for the church around the world, as well as for me personally, is astounding. It helped me realize that when God prompts us to take action, such as making a phone call at a particular moment, we should respond. I shall be forever thankful that Brian Stiller responded to the prompting of God in his life.

Brian Stiller has subsequently told me how thankful he is that he responded to the prompting of God to make that call. Had he ignored the Lord's leading to him at that time, it is frightening to think what might have happened to WEF.

Also, as I reflect on that crucial moment in my own life, I am thankful for the support of a group of godly leaders who joined in earnest prayer. As together we were seeking God's will for the future of WEF, and as I personally sought God's leading for my life, He spoke to the entire group in a way that we could not miss. Scripture tells us that "Plans fail for lack of counsel, but with many advisers they succeed" (Proverbs 15:22 NIV). The encouragement of others was vital to this entire process.

CHAPTER FORTY FOUR
Mission Life Then and Now

"You mean to tell me that you had no air conditioning in that suffocating climate?" That was a common response when friends asked me about the heat in Cartagena, Colombia, where we lived. It is difficult to explain to someone from temperate climates how it feels in the tropics. So my standard reply was to say that there were just a few nights in the year when we felt it necessary to sleep under a sheet. The rest of the year we used no sheet at all. The very thought of a blanket made me itch.

When I reflect on some of the differences that we faced in our years in Colombia, it is almost comical to remember what we had, or did not have, in the way of modern conveniences. Some things taken for granted were unheard of when we lived in Latin America from 1953 to 1968. Here are a few examples.

Telephones—when we lived in Santo Domingo de Heredia in Costa Rica there was one telephone for the entire village. It was located in a pharmacy. If someone called us, which was very rare, the pharmacist had to send a boy to our home nearly half a mile down a dusty lane. If we wanted to make a call, we had to go to the pharmacy.

In Colombia we had a phone in our home for about half the time that we lived there. But in fifteen years in Latin America I can remember only two or three occasions when I made a long distance call to the U.S. This involved going to the central phone office, placing the call, and then waiting for up to five hours for the call to go through, if it went through at all. Today missionaries can keep in touch with friends and family and get through to them immediately.

Whenever I went off into the rural or jungle areas (which was fairly often), it was understood that there would be no communication during that trip, which might be up to several weeks. No one worried that I was out of contact for that period of time. Life went on anyway. My family and my fellow missionaries simply adjusted to the realties of this life.

Computers—the first time I heard the word "computer" it was referred to as an electronic brain. The word "computer" simply was not in our vocabulary. In my administrative work on the field I used an old, stiff typewriter. The first time I got an electric typewriter I had a hard time keeping my fingers off of the sensitive keys and adding a lot of letters that did not belong in the document. We never heard of a copy machine, so in order to make copies for other missionaries and officers of the mission, there needed to be up to eight copies made using carbon paper. If there was a typographical error, it meant going back through each of the copies and using whiteout fluid or an eraser to remove the mistake. It also meant inserting a small protective sheet between copies so that erasures didn't mark the copies below. It was slow and meticulous work.

Email—our fastest form of communication with other countries as well as within our country was the cable or telegram. But it was not instantaneous as email is today. My father died on Christmas day of 1963 when I was in Colombia. My sister Elisabeth was in the U.S. at the time and sent me a cable with a short cryptic message that he had died. But there were no further details. I did not receive the cable for two days. Immediately I tried to call my mother by telephone. It took about six hours for the call to go through. When I finally reached my mother, she had just retuned from the cemetery following the interment after the funeral. She was able to give me the details of his death, but obviously there had been no opportunity for me to get back to the U.S. to join her and the rest of the family in this time of grief.

In 1995, just about the time that email was becoming popular, I was called back by Latin America Mission after having served in other organizations. They needed immediate administrative help while the search went on to find a permanent president. I found out that with email the time invested in keeping up with correspondence literally quadrupled. It took me four times as long to cover the mail of each day as it used to take in the days of "snail mail."

In former days it was quite a task for a missionary to write a prayer letter to friends and supporters. The person had to type the letter, then mimeograph the letter, then address and stamp the envelopes then fold and stuff the letters into the envelopes and then seal them before sending the letters out. Today the missionary can type one letter and with the stroke of a key send it off to hundreds of people at one time. This changes both the frequency and content of the letters. Missionaries started writing far more frequently than before and including far more details than would ever have appeared in a prayer letter in the pre-email days.

Since I was president of the mission, everyone put me on his or her list to receive their emails, and I had no choice but to see what they had written even if the content was quite irrelevant to the work. So it took much longer with all the emails to keep up with the daily correspondence.

Laundry facilities—Some time after returning to the U.S., I was talking with a student who was part of the "counterculture generation" He was complaining about how affluent Christians had become and how few people were concerned about the poor. Too much money was being spent on unnecessary gadgets and modern conveniences. I agreed with him and then admitted sheepishly that I had just bought my wife a laundry dryer. It was our first one. We had never had one before.

He said, "You mean you never had a dryer before?" I replied that it had never been possible even though we lived through heavy rainy seasons when we had three small children with the daily routine of washing diapers. There were no disposable diapers in those days. It was difficult if not nearly impossible some days to dry the clothes, especially in the rainy season.

Even though this young man was complaining about people being too affluent, the idea of not having a dryer seemed preposterous to him. For him, a dryer was not a luxury. Not having a dryer was not in his capacity to understand in spite of his criticism of our culture for having too many luxuries.

Food—If my wife wanted to make a coconut cake, she first bought a full coconut. Then she broke it open, dug out the meat, shredded the meat and prepared the cake. Buying a box of shredded coconut or a cake mix with the coconut already in it was simply not available. That's just one example of preparing food on the mission field.

Travel—To reach many of the places I visited in my missionary work sometimes took as much as three days. The first day was spent on a rickety country bus to the end of the road. The second day would be a 10 or 12 hour trip in a dugout canoe with an outboard motor to go upriver. The third day would be by mule or on foot to reach an isolated village to spend time with new believers. Today those same trips can be made in less than an hour by plane or on the faster roads that have penetrated into the forests and jungles.

When I read the stories and biographies of great missionaries such as William Carey, Hudson Taylor and others, I am rebuked to even allow myself to think that our life was somewhat limited. I am humbled as I read what they endured and am thankful for the privileges God has given me as I see His hand at work in other cultures.

Friends sometimes ask if we or our children felt deprived because we didn't have all the niceties of Western culture. No, but we had privileges that few people have today in more advanced cultures. My boys would travel with me into the woods or jungles, ride in dugout canoes, sleep in jungle hammocks, trudge through mud on trails, ride horseback, eat the local food, see alligators in the rivers, monkeys in the forests, colorful parrots winging by overhead. Today some parents spend thousands of dollars to expose their children to a camping experience. For my sons it was a part of normal life.

As I reflect on how different life was in Latin America in those days from what it is today, I realize that we never thought we were deprived. We learned to live with what was available. What today may sound like deprivation was normal life for me at that time. We could not compare the old telephone system with today's cell phones, because there were no cell phones. We could not compare the old, stiff typewriter with today's computers because there were no computers. We could not compare our slow mail system with today's email, because there was no email.

The missionary today faces a totally different situation from what we faced 50 years ago. Society has changed so drastically that it is hard to make a comparison. But today the missionary still faces major adjustments to the deprivations and pressures of life in another culture. The important thing is not to be distressed over what may seem great limitations or deprivations but to learn to use creatively and happily what is available.

The apostle Paul gave a great statement on how he handled such matters. The missionary of every generation does well to apply Paul's example: "...I have learned to be content whatever the circumstances. I know what it is to be in need, and I know what it is to have plenty. I have learned the secret of being content in any and every situation, whether well fed or hungry, whether living in plenty or in want. I can do everything through him who gives me strength" (Philippians 4:11–13 NIV). We experienced the truth of this then; today's missionaries know it too.

CHAPTER FORTY FIVE
On Being a WASP

When I returned from Latin America after 15 years to work with IVCF, the year was the end of 1968. This was the height of the counterculture movement that was going on in the late 1960s and early 1970s. This was when students and others were protesting just about everything in society. Students in general were negative about government, education, society, church, missions and a wide variety of other matters. The protests centered around many social issues such as the war in Vietnam.

One word that was used frequently in those days with a very pejorative meaning was the word WASP. There was something insidiously negative about being a WASP. What does WASP stand for?

W equals white, A and S equal Anglo-Saxon, P equals Protestant. As I began to hear this word being used, always in a negative way, on my return to the United States, I began to wonder why being a WASP was such a bad thing. I was fully aware that I am a WASP but began to ask myself why this is so bad.

As I looked at the composition of the word, it became evident that being a WASP is no different from being in any other ethnic or racial group.

I am white. Why am I white? Who made me white? Did I have any voice in the color of my skin? Obviously not. I am white because God made me white the same way He made anyone else any other color of skin such as black, brown, yellow, red or whatever. Therefore I have no right to rebel again being what God made me.

I am Anglo-Saxon. Why am I Anglo-Saxon? Did I have any choice in this matter? Who made me Anglo-Saxon? Obviously God did. I had no voice in this any more than I had in the color of my skin. Therefore I have no right to rebel against what God has made me in this area.

P for Protestant. Ah, yes, now I do have a choice. God did not make me a Protestant. I have chosen for myself in that area. I could choose to be any other religious category in the world. I could be, if I wanted, a Jew, a Buddhist, a Hindu, a Muslim, an atheist, an agnostic, or any other religious or non-religious stripe. But I have voluntarily chosen to be a Protestant. Let's make the word more limited in meaning and I am an evangelical follower of Jesus Christ. I will not be ashamed of this. I will not apologize for it.

As I put all of this together, I began to ask myself, *"Am I doing right by accepting criticisms about my being a WASP and being given a guilt trip for what God made me and what I have chosen voluntarily to be?"* I was once tempted to write an article entitled, "I am a WASP—and glad of it." I must confess that I didn't quite have the courage to write an article with that title, although I did write an article on that general subject matter. I tried to point out that what I am today is primarily the result of what God made me in His own sovereignty and also what I have chosen to be in terms of my relationship to Him. Therefore I will not accept a guilt trip for being what God made me and what I voluntarily chose to become. When I hear others being accused of being a WASP, my heart goes out to them and I want to say to them, "You have no right to feel guilty for being what God has made you."

However, it is exceedingly important to recognize why the word "WASP" came to have such a pejorative meaning. All of us white Anglo Saxons must recognize what our race and ethnic group has done to other races and groups. The slave trade was developed by WASPs (although Arabs were also deeply involved), and many of the greedy early barons of industry were WASPs.

When people accused me of being a WASP, putting that in a deeply pejorative sense, I had to face the fact that there were reasons why WASP was such a negative term. I may be justified in seeing WASP, in the basic meaning of the words involved, as an acceptable term. However, I dare not deny that what WASPs have done over the centuries has been deeply painful to other races and ethnic societies. Therefore I accept the fact that they have plenty of bases for their reactions.

When the students and others of the counter-culture generation of the late 1960s and early 1970s rebelled against older generations, they had reason to be resentful. They carried their rebellion against the Vietnam War and racism to the streets and campuses of our land. In some cases this rebellion became violent, as they were reacting against the violence of previous generations of WASPs. But we had to try to understand what lay behind this.

I was not always successful in these efforts, but I think I tried hard to learn. The offices of IVCF were in Madison, Wisconsin, just two blocks from the campus of the University of Wisconsin. Social scientists of that period generally point to that university as being second only to the University of California in Berkeley in the violence of its student rebellions. The campus and local police, backed up by the National Guard, became deeply involved in trying to control this violence.

Because our offices were right in the middle of this, I purposely went out onto the campus of UW to intermingle with students, listening to them, questioning them and trying to identify with their struggles. In the process I experienced the effects of tear gas, which is more drastic than I had realized when only seeing it on TV. I saw the searchlights identifying gatherings and then the billy clubs being swung to break up crowds of which I was a part.

All of this forced me to realize that while I will not accept a guilt trip for being what God has made me and what I have voluntarily chosen to be, I must accept the fact that words can take on further and more sinister meanings in the light of history. This is the fate of being a WASP.

CHAPTER FORTY SIX
We Are Who God Made Us to Be

One of the exhortations constantly given to cross-cultural missionaries is the importance of adapting to the culture. Hudson Taylor, the great missionary to China and founder of the China Inland Mission, adapted to Chinese culture by adopting Chinese dress and a pigtail for his hair. This is often given as a good example of one step in acculturation.

However, missionaries must also realize that there are limits to how well one can adapt to the culture. My sister, Elisabeth Elliot, went to the Waodani Indians in Ecuador after they had murdered her husband, Jim. Questions of adapting to their culture became uppermost in her thinking. Here are a few examples of how she could not adapt fully to their culture.

First, she is a WASP. She is five feet nine inches tall, blond hair, blue eyes, white skin. The Waodani are about five feet tall, black hair, black eyes, bronze skin. Elisabeth could not hide what she is biologically. She stood out among them.

Next, how does one adapt to the culture in terms of dress when the local culture uses no western clothing at all? Elisabeth could not adapt in this area.

The Waodani gave her a house like theirs, which was a roof with no walls. She lived in that house for nearly a year, being exposed 24 hours a day to the entire tribe with peering eyes. We Westerners never think of the need for walls since we never experienced living without them. But Elisabeth finally began to realize how important walls are to our culture. Never having any sort of privacy, day or night, began to wear on her in such a way that she realized that for her own emotional stability, she must have some semblance of privacy. She finally asked the Quechua Indians, with whom she had previously worked and who have walls, to come and build walls for her house.

Each morning she went down to the river to brush her teeth. Many from the tribe followed her to watch this interesting exercise each day. She did not want them to think that this was some sort of a religious ritual. So she asked herself if she should give up this habit so as to be more like the Waodani, who never brushed their teeth. But she knew that if she stopped brushing her teeth she would lose them. She decided that this was another area where she could not identify with the local culture. There were various other areas where Elisabeth could never fully identify herself with the local culture.

While many missionaries do not face such a stark contrast as she did, all missionaries must realize that there are areas of life beyond which we cannot make changes. A WASP will be a WASP for a lifetime, even if we make as many cultural adaptations as possible. We can never change our biological and ethnic roots, so we will always stand out as foreign to another culture.

One time, in a period of less than a year, I had to deal with two missionaries who were trying hard not to be what God had made them. Both were WASPS—white, Anglo Saxon, blond-haired, blue-eyed North Americans. One was a new missionary with only a few months on the field. The other was a veteran of 25 years.

The new missionary was from Alabama and had reacted strongly against the racial treatment of African-Americans in her home state. She had attended the University of Alabama when it had been racially integrated and had experienced the riots that resulted at that time. Within this context she felt that all of us missionaries had failed miserably in relating properly to the Colombians. She was determined to show us how it should be done.

Her method was to marry a Colombian and thus to become Colombian. In a four- month period she came to my office three times to tell me that God was leading her to marry a certain Colombian. Each time, however, it was a different man, and each time he was racially darker than the previous one. Within six months her efforts to become something she could never become, because of what God had made her biologically, caused impossible internal tensions within herself. The result was a total emotional and physical breakdown. We had to send her back to the U.S., and she never returned to the field.

The veteran missionary, after 25 years of fruitful ministry and beloved by all the Colombians, decided, like the young missionary, that we were all badly mistaken. She decided that she must become more "Colombian." Her method was to start attacking all of us North American missionaries so that the Colombians would see that she really was one of them instead of what God had made her. Her attacks on her fellow missionaries took us all by surprise and astounded the Colombians, who had loved her deeply. They were utterly puzzled by her efforts and would ask such things as, "What gives with her? We have always loved and admired her. We cannot understand why she has suddenly changed and is pretending to be someone else."

The tensions she built up within herself were so intense that she also was too distraught emotionally and physically to continue her effective work. Unfortunately she had to return to the U.S. and was never able to complete her ministry in Colombia.

My point in bringing up these cases is to emphasize that none of us can become biologically, racially, or ethnically, something God did not make us to be. We must accept what He made us. We can then relate to other cultures within these limitations in a constructive and positive way.

Needless to say, we must make every effort possible to adapt. We should learn the language, the culture, the music, the folklore, the habits, the history and every other possible area to the best of our ability. But in the final analysis we will always be what God originally created us to be, and we should not try to deny that.

CHAPTER FORTY SEVEN
The Place of Laughter

Laughter is one of the greatest gifts that God has given to His people. There are times when laughter is exactly what the wounded spirit needs. God has gifted some people with the special ability to see humor in the events and things that happen around them and to make other people laugh.

Laughter was a basic element in the Howard family. I was privileged to grow up in a home with several family members who were gifted with humor. Our father had a dry sense of humor. His humor was usually based on the twist of a word that would be unexpected in the immediate context. He would send us into gales of laughter. We still quote some of his classic lines.

Our oldest brother, Phil, is a superb linguist with the ability to imitate the accents of other people. One of the memories we have is his entertaining the family in the evenings. He would pick up the local paper and begin to read it. At each paragraph he would change the accent. It might start with the accent of a New Yorker from Brooklyn. Next he would be in Alabama or Georgia as a southerner. Then he would go to New England and speak as someone from Maine or New Hampshire. Then he would go to Scotland or Ireland or England and on into Italy and the European countries, each time imitating to perfection the accent of that region. He would have the entire family roaring with laughter.

My sister Ginny, while not quite the clown that some of her brothers are, also has a wonderful sense of humor. Like me, she may not be the initiator of hilarity, but she has a spontaneous laugh which responds instantly and heartily to the humor being generated by others in the family. Like her mother, she tends to get utterly dissolved in laughter. This stood her in good stead when she spent twenty-three years as a missionary in the Philippines, raising a family and translating the New Testament into one of the languages of that land.

Our sister Elisabeth is also very good at imitation. She could give entire readings of such things as an English kindergarten teacher talking to her pupils, dealing with the shenanigans of the children and with interruptions from outside the classroom. All this would be done in the most perfect British accent.

This gift that Elisabeth had was used by God in Ecuador, where she learned Spanish with perfection and did translation work in several different indigenous languages including that of the Colorado Indians, the Quichua tribe and the Waodani, who had killed her husband, Jim.

Our brother Tom is the true humorist of the family. He is the funniest man I have ever known. A brilliant scholar with a PhD from New York University, a professor of English literature at college and seminary level, and an author, he could hardly speak a paragraph without inserting, often unconsciously, something that would send his hearers into gales of laughter. When our mother, in her later years, lived in an apartment in Tom's home, he told me that he decided it was his duty to visit her every day and make her laugh. He would visit with her, and before long Mother was dissolved in laughter.

Tom, and our youngest brother, Jim, grew up together at the tail end of our family of six. Many of their early years were spent rooming and playing together. Today the two of them will often entertain the rest of us with renditions of some boyhood memories or imitations of what they did together. We will usually insist on repetitions of these every time we have a family gathering.

When I was directing the Urbana convention in 1976, we wanted a veteran missionary who could speak on "The Joys of Declaring His Glory." If we mentioned the name of Dr. Eric Frickenberg of India, everyone who knew him would start laughing. He had such a cheerful spirit and the ability to laugh. Paul Little had a wonderful gift of humor. As we worked together in IVCF we sometimes found ourselves in heavy discussions that tended to bog us down. Paul's quick wit and spontaneous humor frequently broke the tension, made us laugh and get back to the discussion with renewed vigor. Horace L "Dit" Fenton is another one with the same gift. This leader of the Latin America Mission could break a serious roadblock during discussions with a spontaneous remark that doubled us up with laughter.

The Bible says, "There is a time for everything...and a time to laugh" (Ecclesiastes 3:14 NIV). And, "A happy heart makes the face cheerful...the cheerful heart has a continual feast...a cheerful look brings joy to the heart" (Proverbs 15:13, 15, 30 NIV). And, "A cheerful heart is good medicine" (Proverbs 17:22 NIV). Even God laughs, "The One enthroned in heaven laughs" (Psalm 2:4 NIV).

The Place of Laughter

When my first wife, Phyllis, died in 2003, I received a total of 620 cards, letters and emails extolling her virtues. One common thread that ran through many of them was a reference to her sense of humor. It was fortunate that she had a good sense of humor, as coming into the Howard family without it could have been agonizing. Laughter is one of those special gifts that God has given to us, especially to those who love Him.

When my brother in law, Jim Elliot, and his four companions were speared to death in the Ecuador jungles by the Waodani Indians, I immediately went down from Costa Rica to be with my sister Elisabeth and the other widows. Needless to say, it was a time of special sadness. The atmosphere in Shell Mera, the base from which the five men had gone into the Waodani territory, was heavy. Four of the five widows had small children, and each was speculating on her future.

As we sat around in the evenings talking about the five men and reminiscing about their lives and ministry, again and again we found ourselves being dissolved in laughter. Stories would be told of these men who were all blessed with a great sense of humor. And this breaking down in hearty laughter was exactly what was needed to break through the heaviness of the time. Several of the widows have told me subsequently that this laughter was the most important element as they coped with the tragic loss they had suffered.

All missionaries will face times of sadness and heaviness in their ministry. There will be a tendency to feel overwhelmed with the pressures of the work. That is when a sense of humor can be wonderfully used of God to slice through the heaviness and bring needed relaxation and refreshment.

Laughter should not be stifled in times of grief. It is a God-given gift to bring joy to the heart. Laugher should be welcomed and cultivated to bring healing to a wounded heart and refreshment to a troubled soul.

CHAPTER FORTY EIGHT
Asking and Answering Questions

Children learn by asking questions. Once I was with my three-year-old grandson when he began to ask me a great variety of questions. I finally decided to time him to see how many questions he could ask in a short period of time. He asked me 21 questions in three minutes, thus an average of seven questions per minute! But he was in the process of learning by asking such questions.

Often as I traveled through the back woods of Colombia, meeting in small villages and homes of new believers, I would be overwhelmed with the questions they would ask. Since most of them had no pastor or missionary or even an older Christian to teach them, they would save up questions until a more mature Christian came to help them. When I was with them they would pepper me with questions, sometimes for hours on end. It was an exhilarating experience. It was also good for me, because in the process of answering questions it made me think through issues. Their questions made me realize what new believers were thinking about. In the process I had to confirm my own faith repeatedly as I tried to answer biblically the questions they raised.

The place of questions in the Christian life is a fascinating study. Jesus Himself often used questions to make His disciples think. For example, "Who do people say the Son of Man is?" (Matthew 16:13 NIV) "You do not want to leave too, do you?" (John 6: 67 NIV).

The apostle Peter seemed to ask more questions than any of the other disciples. For example, "Lord, how many times shall I forgive my brother when he sins against me? Up to seven times?" (Matthew 18:21 NIV). "Peter answered him, 'we have left everything to follow you! What then will there be for us?'" (Matthew 19:27 NIV). "Tell us, when will these things happen? And what will be the sign that they are all about to be fulfilled?" (Mark 13:4 NIV).

There are many other examples of disciples asking as well as answering questions. Peter, again, was usually the one to answer questions. When Jesus asked who people thought He was, it was Peter who answered, "You are the Christ, the Son of the living God" (Matthew 16:16 NIV). When Jesus asked the disciples if they also wanted to leave, it was Peter who answered, "Lord, to whom shall we go? You have the words of eternal life. We believe and know that you are the Holy One of God" (John 6:68–69 NIV).

The apostle Paul tells us that in his early Christian life he asked Peter a lot of questions. "Then after three years, I went up to Jerusalem to get acquainted with Peter and stayed with him fifteen days" (Galatians 1:18 NIV). While Paul does not tell us specifically why he went to see Peter, unquestionably he went there to learn from Peter, who had known the Lord directly as a disciple. Undoubtedly he asked scores of questions during those 15 days. It was good for him in his growth and it was good for Peter to be answering those questions. Thus I have found that in my own personal life both asking and answering questions has been salutary in my spiritual growth.

CHAPTER FORTY NINE
Oh, for a Tape Recorder

There have been times in my life when I learned so much and wished I had a tape recorder with me. Something somebody said should have been recorded for posterity but is now lost forever. One of those times was a simple bag lunch at Trinity Evangelical Divinity School (TEDS).

My son David Jr. teaches Old Testament, and for some years taught at TEDS. One day, David invited me to join a few faculty members at a brown-bag lunch. It turned out to be a wonderful opportunity to listen to some great theological discussions. Present that day were some well-known scholars such as Carl F. H. Henry, Kenneth Kantzer, Gleason Archer and John D. Woodbridge.

It so happened that shortly before that lunchtime I had written a review for the Evangelical Missions Quarterly of a book entitled *Through No Fault of Their Own? The Fate of Those Who Have Never Heard.* It is a compilation of 21 essays by leading evangelical scholars dealing with the problem of the fate of those who have never had an opportunity to hear the gospel. Dr. Kantzer had written the Foreword to the book and Dr. Henry had written the "Concluding Remarks." So I tossed out that issue, and immediately those scholars were off and running while I sat back and listened. For a full hour these scholars contributed their thoughts, challenged one another, interacted and questioned. It was one of the most thought-provoking times I have ever had. But that content is lost. I didn't have a tape recorder.

Another time that I wished that I'd had a tape recorder was a lunch at the Fuller School of World Missions. Two weeks earlier, the Urbana '76 planning committee was discussing the theme of the upcoming convention. It was from Acts 1:8, taking the phrase, "you will be my witnesses in Jerusalem, and in all Judea and Samaria, and to the ends of the earth." But we bogged down on the question of what is "Samaria" to today's university students?

The African Americans on the committee said that "Samaria" today is obviously the African American community. They are part of the United States but they really are not a true part of the country. They are isolated. The Canadian representatives said, "No, 'Samaria' is Quebec. They are part of our country but are excluded from full life in it." The Native Americans argued that their people were the real "Samaria" today. While they were the original inhabitants of our land, they were now isolated from full inclusion in the life of the nation. This discussion went on for nearly four hours. We could not agree on how "Samaria" should be presented.

Now, two weeks later at Fuller, I was at lunch with Donald McGavran, Arthur Glasser, Peter Wagner, Ralph Winter, Charles Kraft and others. I asked them the question we had been struggling with at IVCF about what is our "Samaria" today. These Christian leaders spoke of the anthropological implications for Samaria in biblical times that must be kept in mind today. They talked of the theological, sociological, historical, and contextualization factors to consider, as well as church-growth principles that might be considered in the context of Acts 1:8. After all of this discussion, it seemed wise to change the theme to "Declare His Glory Among the Nations" from Psalm 96:3. But how I wish I had recorded that discussion among these men with such brilliant minds. Their biblical and missiological insights are lost forever.

On a personal note, one other time I wished for a recorder was when Phyllis and I celebrated our fiftieth wedding anniversary in the year 2000. At first we had hoped that we might gather our four children and their spouses and our 13 grandchildren for a time of celebration. However, it soon became evident that this would not be possible. So our children, just the four of them, came to our home to celebrate that weekend with us.

One evening during our time together, each one of the children spoke to us with thoughts that each had prepared ahead of time. They expressed to each of us what they most appreciated about us, their upbringing, our ways of training them and our examples to them. It was a deeply emotional time for Phyllis and me. Afterwards we wished that we had recorded those sentiments so that we could listen to those beautiful thoughts again. Now that Phyllis has preceded me to heaven, I am even sorrier not to have a record of what each of our children said to her as well as to me.

In my work in Colombia, and later traveling extensively around the world, I did not usually carry a tape recorder with me. However, as I have looked back over experiences overseas, I have often wished that I'd had a tape recorder with me to record significant conversations and discussions with local believers or with key worldwide mission leaders. In the rural areas of Colombia I learned a great deal from humble believers who were just beginning their walk with the Lord. I often did make notes in a small pocket notebook, but a tape recorder could have been helpful. The disadvantage of that would have been that the minute I pulled out a tape recorder in the presence of a humble new believer, the chances are good that he or she would become much more cautious in what was being said. I may well have missed a great deal of the content of that discussion. The same could have been true on the worldwide level when I had opportunity to interact with key Christian leaders.

CHAPTER FIFTY
"In the Garden"

It was my privilege to grow up singing at home and in church the many great old hymns of the faith written by such authors as Charles Wesley, Isaac Watts, William Cowper and others. We also sang many of the memorable gospel songs from such writers as Fanny Crosby and Francis Ridley Havergal.

One of the favorites of twentieth-century evangelicals has been "In the Garden," written in 1912 by C. Austin Miles. I could sing this by heart from my earliest years. It has been said that next to "The Old Rugged Cross" this song has been one of the most popular gospel songs ever written.

Unfortunately I used to think of it as being a little too sentimental, even though I liked the melody. However, I will never hear or sing it again without remembering a time when my entire appreciation for that hymn was totally altered.

In 1989 I attended a large conference of Asian evangelical leaders in Manila. We heard some fine preachers and Bible expositors at that gathering. But the session that stood out most in my memory was a brief testimony by a man from China named George Chen. He related to us his experience of recent years in China.

George Chen was imprisoned in China for 18 years for no other reason except that he was a follower of Jesus Christ. The prison camp was very large, with thousands of prisoners. Because George was an acknowledged Christian, he became the object of much ill treatment by the guards. In the crowded conditions of the camp George could never find time to be alone with the Lord. He missed his "quiet time" of prayer and meditation which had been his custom before imprisonment.

Every prisoner was given a daily task to do. The most unpleasant and undesirable job in this large camp was to clean out the camp cesspool every morning. Because the camp was so large the cesspool was not large enough to handle all the sewage that would build up overnight, causing it to overflow. Soon the guards decided that this was the job to give to George, since they wanted to make life as unpleasant for him as possible.

As George related this story he told how each morning, as he approached the cesspool to carry out his duties, he saw that the cesspool had overflowed considerably to the surrounding area. Therefore, in order to reach the pool, he had to wade ankle deep in human sewage.

Then with a big smile on his face George said, "But I came to thank God for this job, because I had something that no one else in camp had. I had *privacy!* No one wanted to be near me either before or after my work. So now I had time alone when I could talk with the Lord."

Then he went on to explain: "So I began to think of that cesspool as my garden, where I could meet alone with the Lord every day. And this became a source of great joy for me. As I waded through human sewage, heading for the cesspool to do my daily task, I would sing:

'I come to the garden alone, while the dew is still on the roses;

And the voice I hear, falling on my ear, the Son of God discloses.

And He walks with me, and He talks with me, and He tells me I am His own;

And the joy we share as we tarry there none other has ever known.'"

Then George sang this song to us in Mandarin and again in English. Suddenly the entire congregation of several thousand people in this congress spontaneously joined him in singing in various languages. The great auditorium rang as this song of thanks welled up in praise to the Lord.

I will never sing that song again without picturing George Chen wading ankle deep through human waste, looking forward to meeting the Lord in "his garden" and singing of the joy he found as he met with the Lord.

CHAPTER FIFTY ONE
Is There Room for Two?

When my wife of 53 years, Phyllis, died suddenly in 2003, I was overwhelmed and devastated. For months, and longer, I walked like a zombie groping my way through the seemingly interminable grief. I felt as though I had been cut in half. The realization that I would never see Phyllis again in this life was almost more than I could cope with. Friends tried to encourage me with words such as, "We know she is better off," and "You will see her again," and I know they meant well. But even though I knew that Phyllis was better off, I felt that I was not.

One day, a friend took me to lunch and said, "Dave, I know to some extent what you are going through. I cannot claim to fully empathize because every situation is different. But I have been through what you are experiencing. I lost my wife seven years ago." But then he added, "I also know the joy of remarriage, as God has brought a wonderful new wife into my life." My reply was, "I cannot imagine how I could ever find another person who would be remotely the perfect wife that Phyllis was." He replied, "You won't. You won't ever find anyone who could replace Phyllis. She was a Cadillac, and you won't find another Cadillac." Then with a sly smile he said, "But you might just find a Porsche."

At that stage, I was not ready even to think about such a possibility. The months passed into another year. Over time I became acquainted with a widow, Janet Kuhns, whose husband died after 42 years of a wonderful marriage. She was leading a bereavement support group for people who were grieving the loss of a spouse or family member. I began attending this class and found it to be very helpful.

Little by little, a friendship began to develop with Janet. We found we had a lot in common, such as comparing her years as a missionary in Indonesia and mine in Colombia. After two years, the Lord made it clear to me that Janet was His choice to restore me to the fullness of a life that had been cut in half. After some ups and downs in my mind, the Lord freed me up to ask Janet to marry me. She very wisely asked, "Why do you want to marry me?" When I told her that I loved her and added other reasons, she accepted my proposal.

In my daily devotions, I use the *Daily Light*. Often the verses of a certain day will be used of God to meet some special need in my life. So I will sometimes jot a note in the margin giving the year when this portion of Scripture helped me, and a brief explanation of why the section helped me at that time. I have two notes for September 6. One says, "2004, one year after the death of Phyllis." She had died on September 6, 2003. The other says, "2005, first day in new home with Janet." Janet and I were married on August 27, 2005, just two years after the death of Phyllis.

One of the struggles I had when my friendship with Janet was developing was this: "Is it possible to have room in my heart to love two women? Would I have to forget my 53 years of love for Phyllis in order to love Janet, my new wife?" As I thought about this, I was reminded of Psalm 4:1. Years before a dear friend had encouraged me with this verse when I was struggling through some deep waters. He drew my attention to one phrase which reads, "Thou hast enlarged me when I was in distress" (KJV), and "Thou hast given me room when I was in distress" (RSV). Another rendering reads, "Amidst distress thou hast ever granted me enlargement."

I was able to see that God could enlarge me and give me more room in the midst of my distress. God was graciously enlarging me, giving me room in my heart for two. I did not have to stop loving Phyllis. Rather, in the midst of my distress over the loss of my first wife, God would use even that distress to enlarge my heart to make my heart large enough to encompass a new person in true love. These two women, although totally different in personality and looks, have both been God's clear choice to me. While I was married to Phyllis there was no room in my heart for another. But when Phyllis was taken from me, in the midst of my deep distress God enlarged my heart, making room for Janet, my new and beloved wife.

CHAPTER FIFTY TWO
God's Encouragement to Me

My wife, Janet, spent 40 years in Indonesia with her husband, Bill Kuhns, as missionaries with The Christian and Missionary Alliance. She was a part of that denomination from her earliest days, as her father had been a pastor and a key leader of that denomination. My church background was not from the C&MA. However, over the years I had many excellent contacts with them in my work in Colombia and elsewhere. I considered myself to be a good friend of many Christian and Missionary Alliance people.

After we were married, I was able to attend the 2009 General Council of the C&MA with Janet. This conference is held every two years. While there, I met many pastors, missionaries, lay leaders and other friends of the C&MA. This was a delightful experience for me. One of the amazing and even startling things for me during that General Council was to meet various people who expressed appreciation to me for the influence I apparently had had on their lives even though I did not know it.

On our first day at the Council I met one of the vice presidents of the C&MA. He immediately expressed to me deep appreciation and thanked me so much for my influence on him. I had never heard of this particular man. He told me that he had attended Urbana '76, where I was the director. He told me that at that convention, while he was a student, God spoke to his heart and he committed himself to missions. The result was that he had spent the rest of his life up to that time serving God in overseas outreach under the auspices of The Christian and Missionary Alliance.

One day in the course of that week, Janet and I were walking through the convention hall when a lady came directly toward us. She suddenly stopped and called out in surprise, "Dave Howard! I am delighted to see you!" I had no idea who she was and had no recollection of having seen her before. She immediately began to explain that she had attended a conference at a large family camp in upstate New York known as Camp of the Woods. I was a speaker during the week she was there. Every morning we had a chapel service. Throughout that week I had spoken on the life of the apostle Paul.

She explained to me in intricate detail that the fourth message of that week touched her heart so deeply that her whole life had been turned around and she had found new joy in life in Jesus Christ. That particular message, according to her, was about one aspect of the life of Paul. Well, to my knowledge, I had never seen the woman before. Certainly I had no recollection of her. Somehow God had taken the Word of God spoken through me and used it to speak to her heart.

Also, during that same week, a young fellow jumped up in front of me, called out to me excitedly, and told me that he was a 1993 graduate of Wheaton College. He explained that while he was a student at Wheaton, I had been a speaker there for a week of special meetings. During that week God used those messages to touch his heart. I had apparently told some stories about what God did during my days at Wheaton College as a member of the class of 1949.

Our class was used of God in remarkable ways in subsequent years. Some of our class members became well-known Christian leaders. Two of them were Jim Elliot and Ed McCully, who were among the five martyrs who were killed by the Waodani Indians in the jungle of Ecuador in 1956. Jim Elliot had been a key campus leader, especially in the Student Foreign Missions Fellowship, and Ed McCully had been our senior class president as well as an outstanding athlete in football and track. Other leaders of our class included such men as Larry Ward, the founder of Food for the Hungry; Arthur Johnston, who founded a theological seminary in Amsterdam; Bob Mitchell, who served as president of Young Life; Bill Starr, who also served as president of Young Life; and others who made great contributions in the field of Christian leadership. Actually, all four of the class presidents of the class of 1949 went to the mission field. The freshman president went to Africa, the sophomore president went to Latin America, the junior president went to Taiwan and the Philippines, and the senior president went to Ecuador.

When I met this young man, he was so intrigued with the class of '49 that he wanted to pick my brains and learn all he could about that class. During the course of that week he and I had several fascinating visits together as he expressed his deep desire to know the Lord better and be encouraged and helped by the testimony of others.

My entire experience that week at the C&MA General Council was a time of great encouragement for me. It showed how God can use us in ways of which we might be totally oblivious. I was encouraged that testimonies such as these, some that went back as much as 60 years in time, were used of God to encourage my own heart in the ministry. It is as though God is letting me know that He has been at work in and through my life and that He wanted to give me just a glimpse of His work in me. It certainly causes me to praise Him more as I reflect back on what God has done through my life.

CHAPTER FIFTY THREE
Changes in Missions

I have been involved in missions for more than half a century. The changes I've seen over the years have been seismic and volcanic. For example:

There were the changing student generations. The World War II generation was different from any previous or subsequent generation of students. When the U.S. Government passed the G.I Bill of Rights at the end of the war, any person who had served in the military was entitled to attend college or trade school at government expense. The colleges were flooded with millions of men and women, many of whom, for financial reasons, would not have been able to attend college previously.

This meant that the post World War II student population was older than previous or subsequent ones. Most were in their 20s and 30s. Because of age and war experience, these students were more serious about life than the usual freshman students. They had faced death and had a far deeper appreciation of life. They had seen buddies blown to pieces in front of their eyes. Many of them had been wounded, and they struggled across campus on crutches or artificial limbs. So while they were cheerful, they also had a serious side.

Those men and women had a greatly expanded view of the world; the Christian veterans had a larger view related to missions. They had seen the world as no previous generation had seen it. They had seen such destruction that many Christian students had a desire to go back and restore and give the gospel to those lands. They were founding new mission societies with this aim in view.

Mission Aviation Fellowship was founded by pilots who had flown the bombers and fighter planes during the war. Their attitude was, "Uncle Sam taught us to fly; now let's put that skill to work on behalf of missions. We can fly missionaries to their remote outposts faster than they can get there by any other mode of travel." They knew that one minute of flying time was equivalent to one hour on foot.

Greater Europe Mission was founded by men who had fought through Europe and wanted to go back as missionaries to those devastated lands. Far Eastern Gospel Crusade, now known as SEND International, was founded by GIs who, while in the occupation forces, founded a Bible institute and seminary in the Philippines and a gospel radio ministry in Japan.

The attitude of society in those days was for lifelong commitment, no matter what field or profession one intended to enter. Men and women entering missions expected to spend their lives serving in the land where they went. There was no thought of short-term missions. It was a commitment for life. Those veterans had a profound influence on us younger students. They had seen the world and had acquired a vision for the world that previous generations did not have. They challenged us to reach out to the world that they had seen.

There was the slowly changing adherence to Indigenous Church Principles. In the middle of the nineteenth century, three mission leaders, each independently of the others, came up with three principles that became known as the "Indigenous Church Principles." These men were Henry Venn (1796-1873) of the Church Missionary Society of England; Rufus Anderson (1796-1880) of the American Board of Commissioners for Foreign Missions; and John Nevius (1829-1893), Presbyterian missionary to China and Korea. Their concept was that churches founded by missionaries from a foreign culture must become "self-supporting, self-governing and self-propagating."

For the next hundred years, most mission societies paid lip service to these principles and would claim that their work was faithful to those concepts. However, the reality was that very few truly adhered to those principles. They were sometimes referred to as "the most talked about but least practiced principles in missions." Autonomy was usually (albeit slowly) given to local churches, but institutions such as hospitals, seminaries, publishing houses, camp grounds and other ministries were seldom totally turned over to national leadership without mission governance or financial support of any kind.

This was true well into the latter half of the twentieth century. Thankfully, I have seen major changes in this area in more recent years as mission societies are turning over complete control of all ministries to national leadership. This is an encouraging trend, even though there is still much to be done by missions in this area.

A corollary to this is how to help the national church develop true independence without producing dependency on the mission society. Most missions have the best motives in wanting to help the national church, especially in less-developed countries where finances are a major problem. Hearts are torn to see the tragic effects of poverty and corruption in so many places. The desire to continue to provide needed help is admirable.

That danger of creating dependency is always present. When any church or organization is constantly looking to outside help for the support of their ministries, the temptation to continue helping them because of the need is great. To suggest that such help is creating dependency and therefore should be decreased or eliminated is not popular. The issue has been joined by such groups as World Mission Associates, whose purpose is to help the church in the more affluent countries face up to the dangers of creating dependency in less affluent nations and to help the national churches find their own ways of becoming truly independent. This is one of the biggest issues in missions today.

We are also seeing the changing focus from geography to people groups and the discovery of the 10/40 window concept. The change of focus from missions aiming at geographical areas to targeting people groups is one of the most significant developments of the last quarter of the twentieth century. This important issue was part of the bombshell that was dropped at Lausanne in 1974. It has totally changed our thinking about the unreached peoples of the world.

In 1989, Luis Bush discovered through computer "surfing" that the largest number of unreached people groups was located in the areas between the tenth and fortieth degrees of latitude on the world map. Thus the suggestion was made that mission societies should concentrate on those living and working within that 10/40 window.

There is no doubt that the countries located in that window include the most neglected people who have had slim chance of ever hearing the gospel. Therefore, financial support and missionary presence are being transferred from other areas of the world to ministries within that geographical window.

This makes sense from one perspective. However, there is another side to this coin. Most of Europe is totally secular but is not considered part of the 10/40 window. Latin America is almost totally excluded from that window, as are some other parts of the world. As one whose primary mission experience has been in Latin America, I find myself reacting negatively to the idea that churches should withdraw their support from sending missionaries to Latin America. While many churches in Latin America today are quite capable of standing on their own feet without foreign help, there are still vast unreached peoples in remote tribal groups as well as in large cities through the urbanization flow. Should we in the affluent countries now ignore these areas in favor of concentrating on the 10/40 window?

There is the changing color of world missions. For centuries the mission movement had been from west to east, from Europe, North America and Australia/New Zealand. The church in other parts of the world tended to not recognize or act upon their responsibility to participate in missions. Even within the white nations it did not occur to sending agencies that non-white Christians could be considered for missions.

Fortunately, that is all changing today. Studies show that the missionary force is rapidly changing color and ethnic identity. Nations that once were only on the receiving end of missions are now sending missionaries from their churches to other parts of the world.

We are seeing the need for balance between evangelism and social concerns. In the early decades of the twentieth century there was a great rift between the so-called "modernists" and "fundamentalists." The primary issue was whether the church's responsibility was to preach the simple gospel or to care for the physical and social needs of people. It was tragic because it was based on an either/or situation. It was believed that either we preached the gospel or we got involved in people's social, political and physical needs. But we could not do both.

That rift dominated much of the early twentieth century. It did not really begin to be resolved until the International Congress on World Evangelization held in Lausanne in 1974. A biblically and theologically strong emphasis emerged which turned the tide. Evangelicals began to accept and promote the holistic concept of preaching the gospel with all of its ramifications of love for God and love for our fellow human beings. This has vitally changed the emphasis and ministry of most missions of good repute.

There is the trend to urbanization and globalization. Most sociologists, whether secular or religious, are aware of the great global movement from rural to urban societies. Great masses of people are moving from agriculture to the cities and industry. Missions have thus been forced to develop new strategies of urban evangelism as distinct from the traditional rural work that characterized much of the earlier missionary movement.

At the same time we are becoming increasingly conscious of living in a global society. As far back as 1940, Wendell Wilkie, a presidential candidate, wrote a book entitled *One World*. It showed that we cannot live in isolation from the rest of the world.

There is also the church growth movement. It was Donald McGavran, in his 1955 publication *The Bridges of God*, who pioneered the church growth movement that has characterized much of the mission scene ever since. Missionaries, mission leaders, missiologists and theologians all see the value of this emphasis in getting back to the heart of the gospel and working for the growth of the church. This has been overwhelmingly influential on missionary thinking and practice. Dr. McGavran has had many disciples who have expanded and elaborated on his vision and pioneering work. There have been some skeptics, but changes in missionary work have come from his initiative.

We are contextualizing our gospel, ourselves and our ministries. The apostle Paul was the first to emphasize the need for contextualizing the message of the gospel, though not the content of the gospel. He said, "Though I am free and belong to no man, I make myself a slave to everyone, to win as many as possible. To the Jews I became like a Jew, to win the Jews. To those under the law I became like one under the law…so as to win those under the law. To those not having the law I became like one not having the law…so as to win those not having the law…I have become all things to all men so that by all possible means I might save some" (1 Corinthians 9:19–22 NIV).

Paul's idea was that he had to fit as well as possible into the culture and understanding of those he wished to win to Christ without sacrificing the heart of the gospel. Today this has become a fully accepted concept, but it was only in more recent decades that this has been true.

In recent years the concept of contextualizing both oneself and one's ministry has been a growing and strong emphasis in mission circles. When I was a missionary candidate, as well as in my early years in missions, we never heard the word "contextualization." But it has become a watchword in missiological studies in the last few decades. It is an important and valuable concept

Now there are the building pressures between Islam and Christianity. In my younger years, especially in Latin America, we thought we faced two ideologies opposed to the gospel, Roman Catholicism and Communism. Today, with the collapse of Communism in many parts of the world, this is no longer the threat that we once felt it was. As for Roman Catholicism, I saw great suffering by the evangelicals in Latin America, especially in Colombia where I worked. There was much persecution, including the torture and killing of Protestants by the Roman Catholic hierarchy in those days.

However, since then I have also seen the positive changes made in the treatment of Protestants by Catholics as a direct result of Vatican II. The entire attitude of the Roman Catholic Church changed dramatically as a result of the teaching of Pope John XXIII. Today, while there are still some pockets of persecution in Latin America, these are far fewer and more isolated than previously. Relationships in general are positive and friendly.

Now we are facing the threat of Islam to the gospel of Jesus Christ. There has always been persecution of Christians in some Islamic countries. Historically, the Crusades throughout the Middle East place plenty of fault on both sides to satisfy critics from any angle. But today the story is different. Increasingly we are faced with the openly declared goal of Islamic terrorists to conquer and rule the world. The goal of the suicide bombers and the terrorists who train, control and send them is unmistakable.

The implications in this worldwide threat of Islam seem far more serious for Christian missions than did the threat of Communism a few years ago. Having carefully read every page of the Koran, I am convinced that the fanatical terrorists believe they are doing exactly what the Koran orders them to do, which is to eliminate the "infidels." Promises of paradise are given to any who die in Jihad. The moderate Muslims, many of whom are fine citizens, are not following the commands of the Koran to eliminate the infidel.

Therefore, today Christian missions are faced with a new and, in some ways, a far more menacing enemy than ever before. Part of the danger is that so many in our society do not see Islam as a threat. Much of the media prefers to promote Islam as a "religion of peace." Yet the word "Islam" does not mean peace, except through surrender and submission. Once all are Muslims, there will be "peace." History will tell the final story, but I feel that this present threat could be the greatest the Church of Jesus Christ has ever faced.

I have seen many changes in my more than half-century of being involved in missions and observing the changing face of missions. These changes will continue. But I am unashamedly an optimist and a theological "triumphalist" when I look to the future. I love the great declaration in Revelation 11:15 which reads, "The kingdom of the world has become the kingdom of our Lord and of his Christ, and he will reign for ever and ever" (NIV).

INDEX
Some of the Books That Have Especially Influenced Me.

Books on my relationship with God:
Shadow of the Almighty by Elisabeth Elliot

The biography of Jim Elliot struck deep into my heart. Jim had been my best friend in college. When we lived together in the dormitory at Wheaton College, Jim began to keep journals which later became famous and were often quoted. He tried to persuade me to do the same, saying, "Dave, we are learning so much about God that we should not let it slip away. I'm going to keep a journal and you should do the same." To my regret, I did not take his advice at that time.

Later, when I read his biography and found comments about me and our growing relationship to God, I was keenly disappointed that I had no record of how I was responding to God at that time. I started keeping a journal many years later, but it was too late to recover the lessons of college days with Jim. But his writings challenged me to a new level of commitment.

The Baptism and Fullness of the Holy Spirit, by John R.W. Stott

During our years in Colombia the Holy Spirit began a wonderfully deep and abiding work among uneducated believers in remote areas of the forest. It was exciting to see the spontaneous combustion of a growing church.

Along with this explosive growth came a new emphasis on the gifts of the Spirit. This began to polarize the older and the newer churches. The older, more conservative churches felt that the "wild fire" sweeping through newer areas was not from the Lord. Those who were swept up in this fire felt that this was the only way to worship God and that the older churches were anti-Holy Spirit.

As missionaries, we got caught in the middle. I was especially targeted from both sides because I served as Field Director of the Latin America Mission. In my personal life I had never experienced some of the more visible gifts of the Spirit that were now being manifested among Colombian believers.

John Stott's book was published when I was at the height of personal and spiritual confusion about this. His balanced and thoroughly biblical view of this area of life settled my mind and allowed us to help the churches work through this theological minefield. John Stott offered theological perspicuity and remarkable gifts of articulation on this subject.

Books on Public Ministry:

Two books by Alexander Whyte were especially challenging to me for public ministry of the Word of God.

Lord, Teach Us to Pray introduced me to Whyte's writings and his way of expositing Scripture with a holy imagination. This is a series of messages on prayer, all of which challenged my prayer life.

Bible Characters opened up new vistas for me in studying the characters of the Bible and how they relate to God. As a result, I found myself preaching for many years from character studies in the Bible. As many as 50 years later, friends have told me that they still remember a series of messages on Bible characters that I had given. This has been gratifying to me.

Books on Mission Administration:

The Bridges of God, by Donald McGavran

This was the first of many books by Dr. McGavran that significantly influenced the missions movement for many years. He was "the father of the church-growth movement." He exposited biblical principles of church growth applied to the history and modern developments in missions which have changed how mission leaders have understood their tasks. This book, as well as others that he wrote, had a great impact on me in my positions of responsibility in the Latin America Mission and elsewhere.

Crusade in Europe, by General Dwight D. Eisenhower

This book is obviously not about evangelical missions, but Dr. Kenneth Strachan, late general director of the Latin America Mission, once said that this was the best book on mission administration that he ever read. This prompted me to read the book, and I found it extremely helpful in my work.

General Eisenhower tells how he planned, organized and carried out the greatest military undertaking in history—the invasion of Normandy in 1944.

His exceptional ability to get widely diverse people and nations to work together is outstanding.

His philosophy of delegation was a major key to his ultimate victory. He insisted that decisions should be made at the lowest level possible, as close to the action as possible. If a decision could be made by a corporal, it should not be made by a lieutenant. He carried this up the line of command through the ranks. This worked both ways. If a decision had to be made by a general, he could not delegate it downward to a lower rank.

I found this to be very applicable to mission administration in my work in such large projects as directing the massive student missions convention of InterVarsity Christina Fellowship. I was grateful for the lessons I learned through this book.

Books on the History of Church and Missions:
Christianity Through the Centuries, by Earle E. Cairns

Dr. Cairns fanned into flame my interest in church and mission history through his course on this topic at Wheaton College Graduate School. His encyclopedic grasp of historical facts and his ability to develop the entire movement of the church over the centuries was magnificent.

From Jerusalem to Irian Jaya: A Biographical History of Christian Missions, by Ruth Tucker

Ruth Tucker's approach to the history of missions was creative. Instead of tracing through history the movements themselves, she did it through the biographies of great mission leaders from the first century onwards. This readable and enjoyable book fit well in my area of ministry.

Books on My Relationship to the World and Society:
Child of the Dark, by Carolina Maria de Jesus

This is the diary of a woman who lived in the "favelas," the lowest of the slums in the megacity of Sao Paulo, Brazil. She relates day by day what she had to do to feed her starving children and to survive herself. Daily grubbing through garbage pits to find bits of food or discarded items such as cardboard that she could sell for a few pennies is one of the most heart-rending stories I have ever read. It is not fiction. These are true-life accounts of a woman who refused to beg and insisted that she would survive somehow by her own efforts. It was the greatest introduction to me of what the poor of this world live with every day of their lives.

The Autobiography of Malcolm X
This book introduced me to the thinking of one of the most influential leaders of modern times in the area of racial conflict. The bitterness of the author, coupled with the reality of what he says, shocked and disturbed me. But it opened my eyes to the feelings of a whole segment of society that I had ignored. After reading this book I could never be the same in my feelings about those from another ethnic, racial or religious background.

Books about Human Achievements:
The Endurance: Shackleton's Legendary Antarctic Expedition, by Caroline Alexander
This 1914 expedition was one of the most heroic in all the history of explorations around the world. What Sir Ernest Shackleton and his men endured and ultimately survived is almost beyond belief. I have read the book twice and probably will read it again.

Undaunted Courage: Meriwether Lewis, Thomas Jefferson, and the Opening of the American West, by Stephen E. Ambrose
This is the famous story of the Lewis and Clark expedition up the Missouri River and on to the west coast. To me it is a page-turner almost unequaled in the annals of great explorations.

Nothing Like It In the World: The Men Who Built the Transcontinental Railroad 1863–1869, by Stephen Ambrose
Until I read this book I had not realized that the transcontinental railroad was one of Abraham Lincoln's top priorities even at the height of the devastating Civil War. He felt that just as keeping the North and South together was indispensable for the survival of the Union, so linking east and west together was equally essential to building a strong nation. The story of how Lincoln insisted that this must be done, even during the bloody conflict, and how the largely Chinese and Irish immigrants carried it out through harrowing dangers, is breathtaking.

The Path Between the Seas: The Creation of the Panama Canal 1870-1914, by David McCullough
Detailing one of the most difficult enterprises in the history of the western hemisphere, this book carries the reader along at an exciting pace.

Some of the Books That Have Especially Influenced Me.

Men to Match My Mountains: The Monumental Saga of the Winning of America's Far West, by Irving Stone

I enjoy reading books like this from well-established authors. It is written in fascinating prose.

The Discoverers: A History of Man's Search to Know His World and Himself, by Daniel J. Boorstin

This book covers discoveries in the history of the universe in such areas as Time, Earth and the Seas, Nature, Science Goes Public, Inside Ourselves, Cataloguing the Whole Creation, Society, Opening the Past, Surveying the Present. The author was the Librarian of Congress, Senior Historian of the Smithsonian Institution and Director of the National Museum of History and Technology. A graduate of Harvard and Yale, and a Rhodes scholar at Oxford, he taught at the University of Chicago, the Sorbonne and Cambridge University. It would be hard to find a scholar more qualified to write on such sweeping subjects. He does it well, and I found it utterly intriguing.

Other Books on History:

Modern Times: The World from the Twenties to the Nineties, by Paul Johnson

Since this was the period of time in which I grew up, went to school, went into missions, reared my family and served the Lord in a variety of positions around the world, it is natural that I should be interested in what was going on in the world of my lifetime. This book is one of those that I especially appreciate.

The American Revolution, by Bruce Lancaster

From my early school days the stories of our founding fathers, and the revolution that they carried out, has always fascinated me. That's why I found this book that was published in 2001 to be educational for me.

The Singapore Story: From Raffles to Lee Kwang Yew, by Noel Barber. Since I lived in Singapore from 1987 to 1992, I did extensive reading on the history and culture of that amazing country. This fairly short but exciting book was one of the best I read during those years.

The Greatest Generation, by Tom Brokaw

Since I was born at the tail end of this generation, I cannot claim to be one of the heroes who endured the Great Depression, won the greatest war in history and built a new and amazingly successful nation after the war. However, because I grew up during that period of time, I find myself resonating with the writing on every page of Brokaw's gripping book.

Flags of Our Fathers, by James Bradley

Most Americans know the famous war photo taken of the raising of the American flag on the summit of Mt. Suribachi on Iwo Jima during one of the bloodiest battles of World War II. This absorbing book traces the life and stories of the six men who raised that flag. Few stories out of that war are more captivating.

Biography:

Biographies have always interested me. It is helpful to see what others have learned in life, how God worked in them, how circumstances, culture, politics, society and many other factors shaped them, and how they responded. I have read many biographies and mention just a few here as examples.

A Chance to Die: The Life and Legacy of Amy Carmichael, by Elisabeth Elliott

When I was in college, Jim Elliot and I became intensely interested in the poems as well as the prose of this great missionary who spent more than fifty years in India rescuing temple prostitutes and writing of an intimate walk with God. When my sister wrote Amy Carmichael's biography, I found it especially absorbing.

Bold As a Lamb: Pastor Samuel Lamb and the Underground Church in China, by Ken Anderson

The story of the house-church movement in China during the last half of the twentieth century has always enthralled me. When my wife, Phyllis, and I had the opportunity of meeting Pastor Lamb, one of the great leaders of this movement, in his home in China, I was thrilled. His story, both in person and in this book, has been a great challenge to me.

Who Shall Ascend: The Life of R. Kenneth Strachan of Costa Rica, by Elisabeth Elliot

One of the gratifying privileges of my life was to work directly under Dr. Strachan as one of his assistants in the Latin America Mission. He had a profound influence on my life and thinking. So his biography was especially interesting to me.

Abraham Lincoln: The Prairie Years and the War Years, by Carl Sandburg

This three-volume life story of Abraham Lincoln is a classic that gave me insights into the life and work of one of the greatest men in United States history.

Hudson Taylor and China's Open Century, by A. J. Broomall. This is a seven-volume work on the great missionary to China.

Here I Stand: The Life of Martin Luther, by Roland Bainton.

The impact of Luther on the world is incalculable and his life story is invaluable.

Earl Dix: Adventurer for God, by Earl Young Dix and Bonnie Palmer

Here is the story of an unsung hero. Most of us have never heard of Earl Dix, but he was a remarkable missionary to Africa. I find it encouraging to read biographies of lesser-known saints whose crown of faithfulness in heaven will far outshine the crowns of some far-better-known people.

The Last Lion: Winston Spencer Churchill, by William Manchester

Clearly one of the greatest leaders of the Twentieth Century, Winston Churchill lends himself wonderfully to great biographies. This is one of the best that I have read.

Novels

Novels can be entertaining and instructive when written by competent authors and covering believable life situations. I enjoy novels for relaxation and a change from heavier types of books. Here is a list of some of the authors and their novels that I have enjoyed reading:

Charles Dickens: *Oliver Twist, Bleak House, Great Expectations, Nicholas Nickleby* and *The Old Curiosity Shop*

Victor Hugo: *The Hunchback of Notre Dame* and *Les Miserables*

Willa Cather: *O Pioneers* and *My Antonia*

Leo Tolstoy: *Anna Karenina* and *The Death of Ivan Illyich*

Fyodor Dostoevsky: *The Brothers Karamazov*

Thomas Hardy: *Tess of the d'Ubervilles, The Return of the Native, Far From the Madding Crowd* and *The Mayor of Casterbridge*

John Grisham: A contemporary author who writes spellbinding stories of lawyers and the legal world. I have read most of what he has written and am always entertained by reading them.

One book that doesn't fit into any of the general categories is *The Shaping of a Christian Family* by Elisabeth Elliot. This is the story of our parents, Philip and Katharine Howard. It is honest, humorous, sympathetic and insightful. It does not glorify our parents; rather, it glorifies the Lord who was gracious and merciful to them as they reared their six children. The fact that all six of them entered the Lord's service (four as missionaries, one as a professor in a Christian college and seminary and one who is a pastor) speaks for itself. Needless to say, this book made me even more deeply thankful for my parents.

Epilogue

As I have reflected on all that I saw God do and all of His gracious hand upon my life and the lives of many others, I am humbled and reminded of the words of Moses:

Remember how the Lord your God led you all the way in the desert these forty years (over sixty in my case), *to humble you and to test you in order to know what was in your heart, whether or not you would keep his commands. He humbled you, causing you to hunger and then feeding you with manna, which neither you nor your fathers had known...Your clothes did not wear out and your feet did not swell during these forty years...Observe the commands of the Lord your God, walking in his ways and revering him. For the Lord you God is bringing you into a good land..."*

Deuteronomy 8:2-7 (NIV)

Because all the glory of what is recorded in this book belongs to God, I feel led to share these stories with others who may be blessed in reading them.

One of my favorite hymns, by Joseph Addison (1672-1719), had at least thirteen verses, but I will limit myself at this point to just the first verse.

> "When all thy mercies, O my God,
> My rising soul surveys,
> Transported with the view, I'm lost
> In wonder, love and praise.

Made in the USA
Lexington, KY
12 February 2014